POPULAR SUPERSTITIONS,

AND

THE TRUTHS CONTAINED THEREIN,

WITH AN

ACCOUNT OF MESMERISM.

BY

HERBERT MAYO, M.D.,

FORMERLY SENIOR SURGEON OF MIDDLESEX HOSPITAL; PROFESSOR OF ANATOMY AND PHYSIOLOGY IN KING'S COLLEGE; PROFESSOR OF COMPARATIVE ANATOMY IN THE ROYAL COLLEGE OF SURGEONS, LONDON. F.R.S., F.G.S., ETC.

FROM THE THIRD LONDON EDITION.

WM. S. YOUNG, PRINTER.

PREFATORY REMARKS.

In the following Letters I have endeavoured to exhibit in their true light the singular natural phenomena of which old superstition and modern charlatanism in turn availed themselves—to indicate their laws, and to develope their theory. The subject is so important that I might well have approached it in a severer guise. But, slight as this performance may appear, I profess to have employed upon it the keenest and most patient efforts of reflection of which I am capable. And as to its tone at the commencement, and the prominence given to popular and trivial topics, I candidly avow that, without some such artifice, I doubt whether I should have found a publisher of repute to publish, or a circle of readers to read, my lucubrations.

> "Cosi all' egro fanciul porgiamo aspersi
> Di soave licor gli orli del vaso;
> Succhi amari ingannato intanto ei beve,
> E dall' inganno suo vita riceve."

It was in the winter of 1846 that the original seven Letters were written, of which the present fourteen are the third and expanded reprint. The hour had come for successfully assailing certain already shaking prejudices of the reading public. The Selbstschau of Zschokke, and the researches of Von Reichenbach, were in the hands of the literary and philosophic. The seer-gift of the former (see Letter IV.) had established the fact that one mind can enter into direct though one-sided communion with another. The undenied Od-force of the latter (see Letter I.) is evidently the same influence with that, the first crude announcement of which, by Mesmer, had scared the world into disbelief. It had now become possible to explain ghostly warnings, and popular prophecies, the wonders of natural trance, and of animal magnetism, without having recourse to a single unproven principle. I therefore made the attempt; other more efficient labourers have co-operated in the same object; and public opinion is no longer hostile to this class of inquiries.

BAD WEILBACH, near MAYENCE,
1*st August*, 1851.

CONTENTS.

ON POPULAR SUPERSTITIONS.

LETTER I.

THE DIVINING ROD.—Description of and mode of using the same—Mr. Fairholm's statement—M. de Tristan's statement—Account of Von Reichenbach's Od force—The Author's own observations.

DEAR ARCHY,—As a resource in the solitary evenings of commencing winter, it occurred to me to look into the long-neglected lore of the marvellous, the mystical, the supernatural. I remembered the deep awe with which I had listened, many a year ago, to tales of seers, ghosts, vampyrs, and all the dark brood of night. And I thought it would be infinitely agreeable to thrill again with mysterious terrors, to start in my chair at the closing of a distant door, to raise my eyes with uneasy apprehension towards the mirror opposite, and to feel my skin creep through the sensible "afflatus" of an invisible presence. I entered, accordingly, upon a very promising course of appalling reading. But, a-lack and well-a-day! a change had come over me since the good old times when fancy, with fear and superstition behind her, would creep on tiptoe to catch a shuddering glimpse of Kobbold, Fay, or incubus. Vain were all my efforts to revive the pleasant horrors of earlier years: it was as if I had planned going to a play to enjoy again the full gusto of scenic illusion, and, through absence of mind, was attending a morning rehearsal only; when, instead of what I had anticipated, great-coats, hats, umbrellas, and ordinary men and women, masks, tinsel, trap-doors, pulleys, and a world of intricate machinery, lit by a partial gleam of sunshine, had met my view. The enchantment was no longer there—the spell was broken.

Yet, on second thoughts, the daylight scene was worth contemplating. A new object, of stronger interest, suggested itself. I might examine and learn the mechanism of the illusions which had failed to furnish me the projected entertainment. In the books I had looked into, I discerned a clue to the explanation of many wonderful stories, which I could hitherto only seriously meet by disbelief. I saw that phenomena, which before had appeared isolated, depended upon a common principle, itself allied with a variety of other singular facts and observations, which wanted only to be placed in philosophical juxtaposition to be recognised as belonging to science. So I determined to employ the leisure before me upon an inquiry into the amount of truth in popular superstitions, certain that, if the attempt were not premature, the labour would be well repaid. There must be a real foundation for the belief of ages. There can be no prevalent delusion without a corresponding truth. The visionary promises of alchemy foreshadowed the solid performances of modern chemistry, as the debased worship of the Egyptians implied the existence of a proper object of worship.

Among the immortal productions of the Scottish Shakspeare—you smile, but that phrase contains the true belief, not a popular delusion; for the spirit of the poet lives not in the form of his works, but in his creative power and vivid intuitions of nature; and the form even is often nearer than you think:—but this excursiveness will never do; so, to begin again.

Among the novels of Scott—I intended to say—there is not one more wins upon us than the *Antiquary*. Nowhere has the great author more gently and indulgently, never with happier humour, portrayed the mixed web of strength and infirmity in human character; never, besides, with more facile power evoked pathos and terror, and disported himself amid the sublimity and beauty of nature. Yet, gentle as is his mood, he misses not the opportunity—albeit, in general, he displays an honest leaning towards old superstitions—mercilessly to crush one of the humblest. Do you remember the Priory of St. Ruth, and the summer-party made to visit it, and the preparations for the subsequent rogueries of Dousterswivel in the tale of Martin Waldeck, and the discovery of a spring of water by means of the divining rod?

I am inclined, do you know, to dispute the verdict of the novelist on this occasion, and to take the part of the charlatan against the author of his being; as far, at least, as regards the genuineness of the art the said charlatan then and there affected to practise. There exists, in fact, strong evidence to show that, in competent hands, the divining rod really does what is pretended of it. This evidence I propose to put before you in the present letter. But, as the subject may be entirely new to you, I had best begin by describing what is meant by a divining rod, and in what the imputed jugglery consists.

Then you are to learn that, in mining districts, a superstition prevails among the people that some are born gifted with an occult power of detecting the proximity of veins of metal, and of underground currents of water. In Cornwall, they hold that about one in forty possesses this faculty. The mode of exercising it is very simple. They cut a hazel twig, just below where it forks. Having stripped the leaves off, they cut each branch to something more than a foot in length, leaving the stump three inches long. This implement is the divining rod. The hazel is selected for the purpose, because it branches more symmetrically than its neighbours. The hazel-fork is to be held by the branches, one in either hand, the stump or point projecting straight forwards. The arms of the experimenter hang by his sides; but the elbows being bent at a right angle, the fore-arms are advanced horizontally; the hands are held eight to ten inches apart; the knuckles down, and the thumbs outwards. The ends of the branches of the divining fork appear between the roots of the thumbs and fore-fingers.

The operator, thus armed, walks over the ground he intends exploring, in the full expectation that, if he possesses the mystic gift, as soon as he passes over a vein of metal, or an underground spring, the hazel-fork will begin to move spontaneously in his hands, rising or falling as the case may be.

You are possibly amused at my gravely stating, as a fact, an event so unlikely. It is, indeed, natural that you should suppose the whole a juggle, and think the seemingly spontaneous motion of the divining fork to be really communicated to it by the hands of the conjurer —by a sleight, in fact, which he puts in practice when he believes that he is walking over a hidden water-course, or wishes you to believe that there is a vein of metal near. Well, I thought as you do the greater part of my life; and probably the likeliest way of combating your skepticism, will be to tell you how my own conversion took place.

In the summer of 1843 I dwelt under the same roof with a Scottish gentleman, well informed, of a serious turn of mind, fully endowed with the national allowance of shrewdness and caution. I saw a good deal of him; and one day, by chance, this subject of the divining rod was mentioned. He told me, that at one time his curiosity having been raised upon the subject, he had taken pains to ascertain what there is in it. With this object in view he had obtained an introduction to Mrs. R., sister of Sir G. R., then living at Southampton, whom he had learned to be one of those in whose hands the divining rod moved. He visited the lady, who was polite enough to show him in what the performance consists, and to answer all his questions, and to assist him in making experiments calculated to test the reality of the phenomenon, and to elucidate its cause.

Mrs. R. told my friend that, being at Cheltenham in 1806, she saw, for the first time, the divining rod used by Mrs. Colonel Beaumont, who possessed the power of imparting motion to it in a very remarkable degree. Mrs. R. tried the experiment herself at that time, but without any success. She was, as it happened, very far from well. Afterwards, in the year 1815, being asked by a friend how the divining rod is held, and how it is to be used, on showing it she was surprised to see that the instrument now moved in her hands.

Since then, whenever she had repeated the experiment, the power had always manifested itself, though with varying degrees of energy.

Mrs. R. then took my friend to a part of the shrubbery where she knew, from former trials, the divining rod would move in her hands. It did so, to my friend's extreme astonishment; and even continued to move, when, availing himself of Mrs. R.'s permission, my friend grasped her hands with sufficient firmness to prevent, as he supposed, any muscular action of her wrists or fingers influencing the result.

On a subsequent day my friend having thought over what he had seen, repeated his visit to the lady. He provided himself, as substitutes for the hazel-fork which he had seen her employ, with portions of copper and iron wire about a foot and a half long, bent something into the form of the letter V. He had made, in fact, divining forks of wire, wanting only the projecting point. He found that these instruments moved quite as freely in Mrs. R.'s hands as the hazel-fork had done. Then he coated the two handles of one of them with sealing-wax, leaving, however, the extreme ends free and uncovered. When Mrs. R. tried the rod so prepared, holding the parts alone which were covered with sealing-wax, and walked on the same piece of ground as in the former experiments, the rod remained perfectly still. As often, however, as—with no greater change than adjusting her hands so as to touch the free ends of the wire with her thumbs—Mrs. R. renewed direct contact with the instrument, it again moved. The motion ceased again as often as the direct contact was interrupted.

This simple narrative, made to me by the late Mr. George Fairholm, carried conviction to my mind of the reality of the phenomenon. I asked my friend why he had not pursued the subject further. He said he had often thought of doing so, and had, he believed, mainly been deterred by meeting with the work of the Compte de Tristan, entitled *Recherches sur quelques effluves ter-*

restres, Paris, 1829, in which facts similar to those which he had himself verified were given, and a number of additional curious experiments detailed.

At Mr. Fairholm's instance I procured the book, and, at a later period, read it. I may say that it both satisfied and disappointed me. It satisfied me, inasmuch as it fully confirmed all that Mr. Fairholm had stated. It disappointed me, for it threw no additional light upon the phenomena. M. de Tristan had in fact brought too little physical knowledge to the investigation, so that a large proportion of his experiments are puerile. However, his simpler experiments are valuable and suggestive. These I will presently describe. In the mean time, you shall hear the count's own narrative of his initiation into the mysteries of the divining rod.

"The history of my researches," says M. de Tristan, "is simply this. Some twenty years ago, a gentleman who, from his position in society, could have no object to gain by deception, showed to me, for my amusement, the movement of the divining rod. He attributed the motion to the influence of a current of water, which appeared to me a probable supposition. But my attention was more engaged with the action produced by the influence, let the latter be what it might. My informant assured me he had met with many others in whom the same effects were manifested. When I returned home, and had opportunities of making trials under favourable circumstances, I found that I myself possessed the same endowment. Since then I have induced many to make the experiment, and I have found a fourth, or certainly a fifth, of the number capable of setting the divining rod in motion at the very first attempt. Since that time, during these twenty years, I have often tried my hand, but for amusement only, and desultorily, and without any idea of making the thing an object of scientific investigation. But at length, in the year 1822, being in the country, and removed from my ordinary pursuits, the subject again came across me, and I determined forthwith to try and ascertain the cause of this phenomena. Accordingly, I commenced a long series of experiments, from fifteen to eighteen hundred in number, which occupied me nearly fifteen months. The results of above twelve hundred were written down at the time of their performance."

The scene of the Count's operations was in the valley of the Loire, five leagues from Vendôme, in the park of the Chateau de Ranac. The surface of ground which gave the desired results was from seventy to eighty feet in breadth. But there was another spot equally efficient at the Count's ordinary residence at Emerillon, near Clery, four leagues south of Orleans, ten leagues south of the Loire, at the commencement of the plains of Solonge. The surface ran from north to south, and had the same breadth with the other. These "exciting tracts" form, in general, bands or zones of undetermined, and often very great length. Their breadth is very variable; some are only three or four feet across, while others are one hundred paces. These tracts are sometimes sinuous; in other instances they ramify. To the most susceptible they are broader than to those who are less so.

M. de Tristan thus describes what happens when a competent person, armed with a hazel-fork, walks over the exciting districts:—

When two or three steps have been made upon the exciting tract of ground, the fork, which at starting is held horizontally, with the point forwards, begins gently to ascend; it gradually attains a vertical position; sometimes it passes beyond that, and lowering itself, with its point to the chest of the operator, it becomes again horizontal. If the motion continues, the rod descending becomes vertical, with the point downwards. Finally, the rod may again ascend and resume its first position. When the action is very lively, the rod immediately commences a second revolution; and so it goes on, as long as the operator continues to walk over the exciting surface of ground.

A few of those in whose hands the divining fork moves exhibit a remarkable peculiarity. The instrument, instead of commencing its motion by ascending, descends; the point then becomes directed vertically downwards; afterwards it reascends, and completes a revolution in a course the opposite of the usual one; and as often and as long as its motion is excited, it pursues this abnormal course.

Of the numerous experiments made by M. de Tristan, the following are among the simplest and the best:—

He covered both handles of a divining rod with a thick silk stuff. The result of using the instrument so prepared was the same which Mr. Fairholm obtained by coating the handles with sealing-wax. The motion of the divining rod was extinguished.

He covered both handles with one layer of a thin silk. He then found that the motion of the divining rod took place, but it was less lively and vigorous than ordinary.

By covering one handle of the divining rod, and that the right, with a layer of thin silk, a very singular and instructive result was obtained. The motion of the instrument was now reversed. It commenced by descending.

After covering the point of the divining rod with a thick layer of silk stuff, the motion was sensibly more brisk than it had been before.

When the Count held in his hands a straight rod of the same substance conjointly with the ordinary divining rod, no movement of the latter whatsoever ensued.

Finally, the Count discovered that he could cause the divining rod to move when he walked over a non-exciting surface—as, for instance, in his own chamber—by various processes. Of these the most interesting consisted in touching the point of the instrument with either pole of a magnetic needle. The instrument shortly began to move, ascending or descending, according as the northward or southward pole of the needle had been applied to it.

It is unnecessary to add that these, and all M. de Tristan's experiments, were repeated by him many times. The results of those which I have narrated were constant.

Let me now attempt to realize something out of the preceding statements.

1. It is shown, by the testimony adduced, that whereas in the hands of most persons the divining rod remains motionless, in the hands of some it moves promptly and briskly when the requisite conditions are observed.

2. It is no less certain that the motion of the divining rod has appeared, to various intelligent and honest persons, who have succeeded in producing it, to be entirely spontaneous; or that the said persons were not conscious of having excited or promoted the motion by the slightest help of their own.

3. It appears that in the ordinary use of the divining rod by competent persons, its motion only manifests itself in certain localities.

4. It being assumed that the operator does not, however unconsciously, by the muscular action of his hands and wrists produce the motion of the divining rod, the likeliest way of accounting for the phenomenon is to suppose that the divining rod may become the conductor of some fluid or force, emanating from or disturbed in the body by a terrestrial agency.

But here a difficulty arises: How can it happen that the hypothetical force makes so long and round-about a course? Why, communicated to the body through the legs, does not the supposed fluid complete a circuit at once in the lower part of the trunk?

Such, at all events, would be the course an electric current so circumstanced would take.

The difficulty raised admits of being removed by aid derived from a novel and unexpected source. I allude to the discovery, by Von Reichenbach, of a new force or principle in the physical world, which, whether or not it is identical with that which gives motion to the divining rod, exhibits, at all events, the very property which the hypothetical principle should possess to explain the phenomena which we have been considering.

No attempts have indeed been made to identify the two as one; and my conjecture that they may prove so, should it even appear plausible, is so vague, that I should have contented myself with referring to Von Reichenbach's new principle as to an established truth, and have introduced no account of it into this Letter, had I not a second motive for insuring your cognisance of the curious facts which the Viennese philosopher has brought to light. It is less with the view of furnishing a leg to the theory of the divining rod, than in order to provide the means of elucidating more interesting problems, that I now proceed briefly to sketch the leading experiments made by Von Reichenbach, and their results.

Objections have been taken against these experiments, on the ground that their effects are purely subjective; that the results must be received on the testimony of the party employed; and that the best parties for the purpose are persons whose natural sensibility is exalted by disorder of the nerves; a class of persons always suspected of exaggeration, and even, and in part with justice, of a tendency to trickery and deception. But this was well known to Von Reichenbach, who appears to have taken every precaution necessary to secure his observations against error. And when I add, that many of the results which he obtained upon the most sensitive and the highly nervous, were likewise manifested in persons of established character and in good health, and that the fidelity of the author and of his researches is authenticated by the publication of the latter in Woehler and Liebig's *Chemical Annals*, (Supplement to volume 53, Heidelberg, 1845,) I think you will not withhold from them complete reliance.

In general, persons in health and of a strong constitution are insensible to the influence of Von Reichenbach's new force. But all persons, the tone of whose health has been lowered by their mode of life—men of sedentary habits, clerks, and the like, and women who employ their whole time in needlework, whose pale complexions show the relaxed and therefore irritable state of their frames—all such, or nearly all—evince more or less susceptibility to the influence I am about to describe.

Von Reichenbach found that persons of the latter class, when slow passes are made with the poles of a strong magnet moved parallel to the surface—down the back, for instance, or down the limbs, and only distant enough just not to touch the clothes—feel sensations rather unpleasant than otherwise, as of a light draft of air blown upon them in the path of the magnet.

In the progress of his researches, Von Reichenbach found that the more sensitive among his subjects could detect the presence of his new agent by another sense. In the dark they saw dim flames of light issuing and waving from the poles of the magnet. The experiments suggested by this discovery afford the most satisfactory proofs of the reality of the phenomena. They were the following:—A horse-shoe magnet having been adjusted upon a table, with the poles directed upwards, the sensitive subject saw, at the distance of ten feet, the appearance of flames issuing from it. The armature of the magnet—a bar of soft iron—was then applied. Upon this the flames disappeared. They reappeared, she said, as often as the armature was removed from the magnet.

A similar experiment was made with a yet more sensitive subject. This person saw, in the first instance, flames as the first had done; but when the armature of the magnet was applied, the flames did not disappear: she saw flames still: only they were fainter, and their disposition was different. They seemed now to issue from every part of the surface of the magnet equally.

It is hardly necessary to add, that these experiments were made in a well-darkened room, and that none of the bystanders could discern what the sensitive subjects saw.

Then the following experiment was made:—A powerful lens was so placed as that it should concentrate the light of the flames (if real light they were) upon a point of the wall of the room. The patient at once saw the light upon the wall at the right place; and when the inclination of the lens was shifted, so as to throw the focus in succession on different points, the sensitive observer never failed in pointing out the right spot.

To his new force, which Von Reichenbach had now found to emanate likewise from the poles of crystals and the wires of the voltaic pile, he gave the arbitrary but convenient name of Od, or the Od force.

His next step was to ascertain the existence of a difference among the sensations produced by Od. Sometimes the current of air was described as warm, sometimes as cool. He found this difference to depend upon the following cause: Whenever the northward pole of a magnet, or one definite pole of a large crystal, or the negative wire of a voltaic battery, is employed in the experiment, the sensation produced is that of a draft of cool air. On the contrary, the southward pole of the magnet, the opposite pole of the crystal, the positive voltaic wire, excite the sensation of a draft of warm air.

So the new force appeared to be a polar force, and Von Reichenbach called the first series of the above described manifestations *Od-negative* effects, the second *Od-positive* effects.

From among his numerous experiments towards establishing the polarity of Od, I select the following:—One of the most sensitive of his subjects held, at his desire, a piece of copper wire, by the middle with the right hand —by one end with the left. Then Von Reichenbach touched the free end of the wire with one pole of a large crystal, in order to charge it with Od. The patient immediately felt a sensation in the right hand, which disappeared as quickly, to be felt by the left hand instead, at the further end of the piece of wire. She then was bidden to take hold of the wire with both her hands at the middle, and then to slide them away from each other to the opposite ends: she observed, on doing so, that sensations were produced which were strong and decided when her hands held the two ends of the wire, and diminished in intensity in proportion as the hands were nearer its middle.

Von Reichenbach next came upon the observation that the human hand gives out the Od force; and that the right hand displays the characters of negative Od, the left those of positive Od. The more sensitive subjects recognised, in the dark, the appearance of dim flames proceeding from the tips of his fingers; and all felt the corresponding sensations of drafts of cool or of warm air. Subsequently the whole body was found to share the properties of the hands; the entire right side to manifest negative Od, the entire left side positive Od.

So, in reference to this new force, the human body exhibits a transverse polarity; the condition is thus realized which is required to belong to the hypothetical force through which the divining rod might be supposed to move. If any terrestrial influence were capable of disturbing the Od force in the body, however it might affect its intensity, a current or circuit could only be established through the arms and hands; unless, indeed, some extraordinary means were taken, such as employing an artificial conductor, arched half round the body, to connect the two sides.

The sensations which attend the establishment of a current of Od and interferences with it, in sensitive subjects, are exemplified in the following observations:—

A bar magnet was laid on the palm of the left hand of one of the most sensitive subjects, with its southward pole resting on the end of her middle finger, the northward pole on the fore-arm above the wrist. It thus corresponded with the natural polar arrangement of the Od force in the patient's hand and arm. Accordingly, no sensation was excited. But when the position of the magnet was reversed, and the northward pole lay on the end of the middle finger of the left hand, an uneasy sense of an inward conflict arose in the hand and wrist, which disappeared when the magnet was removed or its original direction restored. On laying the magnet reversed on the fore-arm, the sense of an inward struggle returned, which was heightened on joining the hands and establishing a circuit.

When the patient completed the circuit in another way—namely, by holding a bar magnet by the ends, if the latter were disposed normally, (that is, if the northward pole was held in the left hand, the southward pole in the right,) a lively consciousness of some inward action ensued. A normal circulation of Od was in progress. When the direction of the magnet was reversed, the phenomenon mentioned in the last paragraph recurred. The patient experienced a high degree of uneasiness, a feeling as of an inward struggle extending itself to the chest, with a sense of whirling round, and confusion in the head. These symptoms disappeared immediately upon her letting go the magnet.

Similar results ensued when Von Reichenbach substituted himself for the magnet. When he took Miss Maix's hands in his normally—that is to say, her left in his right, her right in his left—she felt a circulation moving up the right arm through the chest down the left arm, attended with a sense of giddiness. When he changed hands, the disagreeableness of the sensation was suddenly heightened, the sense of inward conflict arose, attended with a sort of undulation up and down the arms, and through the chest, which quickly became intolerable.

A singular but consistent difference in the result ensued when Von Reichenbach repeated the last two experiments upon Herr Schuh. Herr Schuh was a strong man, thirty years of age, in full health, but highly impressible by Od. When Von Reichenbach took his two hands in his own normally, Herr Schuh felt the normal establishment of the Od current in his arms and chest. In a few seconds headache and vertigo ensued, and the experiment was too disagreeable to be prolonged. But when Von Reichenbach took his hands abnormally, no sensible effect ensued. Being equally strong with Von Reichenbach, Herr Schuh's frame repelled the counter-current, which the latter arrangement tended to throw into him. In the first or normal arrangement, the Od current had met with no resistance, but had simply gone its natural course. The distress occurred *from its being felt* through Herr Schuh's accidental sensitiveness to Od; of the freaks of which in their systems people in general are unconscious.

I have concluded my case in favour of the pretensions of the divining rod. It seems to me, at all events, strong enough to justify any one who has leisure, in cutting a hazel-fork, and walking about with it in suitable places, holding it in the manner described. I doubt, however, whether I should recommend a friend to make the experiment. If, by good luck, the divining rod should refuse to move in his hands, he might accuse himself of credulity, and feel silly, and hope nobody had seen him, for the rest of the day. If, unfortunately, the first trial should succeed, and he should be led to pursue the inquiry, the consequences would be more serious: his probable fate would be to fall at once several degrees in the estimation of his friends, and to pass with the world, all the rest of his life, for a crotchety person of weak intellects.

As for the divining rod itself, if my argument prove sound, it will be a credit to the family of superstitions; for without any reduction, or clipping, or trimming, it may at once assume the rank of a new truth. But, alas! the trials which await it in that character!—what an ordeal is before it! A new truth has to encounter three normal stages of opposition. In the first, it is denounced as an imposture; in the second—that is, when it is beginning to force itself into notice—it is cursorily examined, and plausibly explained away; in the third, or *cui bono* stage, it is decried as useless, and hostile to religion. And when it is fully admitted, it passes only under a protest that it has been perfectly known for ages —a proceeding intended to make the new truth ashamed of itself, and wish it had never been born.

I congratulate the sea-serpent on having arrived at the second stage of belief. Since Professor Owen (no disrespect to his genuine ability and eminent knowledge) has explained it into a sea-elephant, its chance of being itself is much improved; and as it will skip the third stage—for who will venture to question the good of a sea-serpent?—it is liable now any morning "to wake and find itself famous," and to be received even at Lincoln's Inn Fields, where its remains may commemoratively be ticketed the Ex-Great-Seal.

Postscript, (1850.)—It may save trouble to some future experimenter to narrate my own exploits with the divining rod.

In the spring of 1847, being then at Weilbach in Nassau, a region teeming with underground sources of water, I requested the son of the proprietor of the bathing establishment—a tall, thin, pale, white-haired youth, by name Edward Seebold—to walk in my presence up and down a promising spot of ground, holding a divining fork of hazel, with the accessories recommended by M. de Tristan to beginners—that is to say, he held in his right hand three pieces of silver, besides one handle of the rod, while the handle which he held in his left hand was covered with a thin silk.

The lad had not made five steps when the point of the divining fork began to ascend. He laughed with astonishment at the event, which was totally unexpected by him; and he said that he experienced a tickling or thrilling sensation in his hands. He continued to walk up and down before me. The fork had soon described a complete circle; then it described another; and so it continued to do as long as he walked thus, and as often as, after stopping, he resumed his walk. The experiment was repeated by him in my presence, with like success, several times during the ensuing month. Then the lad fell into ill health, and I rarely saw him. However, one day I sent for him, and begged him to do me the favour of making another trial with the divining fork. He did so, but the instrument moved slowly and sluggishly; and when, having completed a semicircle, it pointed backwards towards the pit of his stomach, it stopped, and would go no farther. At the same time the lad said he felt an uneasy sensation, which quickly increased to pain, at the pit of the stomach, and he became alarmed, when I bade him quit hold of one handle of the divining rod, and the pain ceased. Ten minutes afterwards I induced him to make another trial; the results were the same. A few days later, when the lad seemed still more out of health, I induced him to repeat the experiment. Now, however, the divining fork would not move at all.

I entertain little doubt that the above performances of Edward Seebold were genuine. I thought the same of the performances of three English gentlemen, and of a German, in whose hands, however, the divining rod never moved through an entire circle. In the hands of one of them its motion was retrograde, or abnormal: that is to say, it began by descending.

But I met with other cases, which were less satisfactory, though not uninstructive. I should observe that, in the hands of several who tried to use it in my presence, the divining fork would not move an inch. But there were two younger brothers of Edward Seebold, and a bath-maid, and my own man, in whose hands the rod played new pranks. When these parties walked *forwards*, the instrument ascended, or moved normally; but when, by my desire, they walked *backwards*, the instrument immediately went the other way. I should observe that, in the hands of Edward Seebold, the instrument moved in the same direction whether he walked forwards or backwards; and I have mentioned that at first it described in his hands a complete circle. But with the four parties I have just been speaking of, the motion of the fork was always limited in extent. When it moved normally at starting, it stopped after describing an arc of about 225°; in the same way, when it moved abnormally at starting, it would stop after describing an arc of about 135°; that is to say, there was one spot the same for the two cases, beyond which it could not get. Then I found that, in the hands of my man, the divining rod would move even when he was standing still, although with a less lively action; still it stopped as before, nearly at the same point. Sometimes it ascended, sometimes descended. Then I tried some experiments, touching the point with a magnetic needle. I found, in the course of them, that when my man knew which way I expected the fork to move, it invariably answered my expectations; but when I had the man blindfolded, the results were uncertain and contradictory. The end of all this was, that I became certain that several of those in whose hands the divining rod moves, set it in motion and direct its motion by the pressure of their fingers, and by carrying their hands nearer to, or farther apart. In walking forwards, the hands are unconsciously borne towards each other; in walking backwards, the reverse is the case.

Therefore, I recommend no one to prosecute these experiments unless he can execute them himself, and unless the divining rod describes a complete circle in his hands; and even then he should be on his guard against self-deception.

Postscript II.—I am now (May, 1851) again residing at the bathing establishment of Weilbach, near Mayence; and it was with some interest and curiosity that the other day I requested Mr. Edward Seebold, now a well-grown young man, in full health, to try his hand again with the divining-rod. He readily assented to my request; and he this time knew exactly what result I expected. But the experiment entirely failed. The point of the divining rod rose, as he walked, not more than two or three inches; but this it does with every one who presses the two handles towards each other during the experiment. Afterwards the implement remained perfectly stationary. I think I am not at liberty to withhold this result from the reader, whom it may lead to question, though it cannot induce myself to doubt, the genuineness of the former performances of Mr. E. S.

LETTER II.

VAMPYRISM.—Tale exemplifying the superstition—The Vampyr state of the body in the grave—Various instances of death-trance—The risk of premature interment considered—The Vampyr visit.

IN acknowledging my former letter, you express an eager desire to learn, as you phrase it, "all about Vampyrs, if there ever were such things." I will not delay satisfying your curiosity, although by so doing I interrupt the logical order of my communications. It is, perhaps, all the better. The proper place of this subject falls in the midst of a philosophical disquisition; and it would have been a pity not to present it to you in its pristine colouring. But how came your late tutor, Mr. H., to leave you in ignorance upon a point on which, in my time, schoolboys much your juniors entertained decided opinions?

Were there ever such things as Vampyrs? *Tantamne rem tam negligenter!* I turn to the learned pages of Horst for a luminous and precise definition of the destructive and mysterious beings whose existence you have ventured to consider problematical.

"A Vampyr is a dead body which continues to live in the grave; which it leaves, however, by night, for the purpose of sucking the blood of the living, whereby it is nourished and preserved in good condition, instead of being decomposed like other dead bodies."

Upon my word, you really deserve, since Mr. George Combe has clearly shown, in his admirable work on the Constitution of Man, and its adaptation to the surrounding world, that ignorance is a statutable crime before nature, and punished by the laws of Providence—you deserve, I say, unless you contrive to make Mr. H. your substitute, which I think would be just, yourself to be the subject of the nocturnal visit of a Vampyr. Your skepticism will abate pretty considerably when you see him stealthily entering your room, yet are powerless under the fascination of his fixed and leaden eye—when you are conscious, as you lie motionless with terror, of his nearer and nearer approach—when you feel his face, fresh with the smell of the grave, bent over your throat, while his keen teeth make a fine incision in your jugular, preparatory to his commencing his plain but nutritive repast.

You would look a little paler the next morning, but that would be all for the moment; for Fischer informs us that the bite of a Vampyr leaves in general no mark upon the person. But he fearfully adds, "it (the bite) is nevertheless speedily fatal," unless the bitten person protect himself by eating some of the earth from the grave of the Vampyr, and smearing himself with his blood. Unfortunately, indeed, these measures are seldom, if ever, of more than temporary use. Fischer adds, "if through these precautions the life of the victim be prolonged for a period, sooner or later he ends with becoming a Vampyr himself; that is to say, he dies and is buried, but continues to lead a Vampyr life in the grave, nourishing himself by infecting others, and promiscuously propagating Vampyrism."

This is no romancer's dream. It is a succinct account of a superstition which to this day services in the east of Europe, where little more than a century ago it was frightfully prevalent. At that period Vampyrism spread like a pestilence through Servia and Wallachia, causing numerous deaths, and disturbing all the land with fear of the mysterious visitation, against which no one felt himself secure.

Here is something like a good, solid, practical popular delusion. Do I believe it? To be sure I do. The facts are matter of history: the people died like rotted sheep; and the cause and method of their dying was, in their belief, what has just been stated. You suppose, then, they died frightened out of their lives, as men have died whose pardon has been proclaimed when their necks were already on the block, of the belief that they were going to die? Well, if that were all, the subject would still be worth examining. But there is more in it than that, as the following o'er true tale will convince you, the essential points of which are authenticated by documentary evidence.

In the spring of 1727, there returned from the Levant to the village of Meduegna, near Belgrade, one Arnod Paole, who, in a few years of military service and varied adventure, had amassed enough to purchase a cottage and an acre or two of land in his native place, where he gave out that he meant to pass the remainder of his days. He kept his word. Arnod had yet scarcely reached the prime of manhood; and though he must have encountered the rough as well as the smooth of life, and have mingled with many a wild and reckless companion, yet his naturally good disposition and honest principles had preserved him unscathed in the scenes he had passed through. At all events, such were the thoughts expressed by his neighbours as they discussed his return and settlement among them in the Stube of the village Hof. Nor did the frank and open countenance of Arnod, his obliging habits and steady conduct, argue their judgment incorrect. Nevertheless, there was something occasionally noticeable in his ways—a look and tone that betrayed inward disquiet. Often would he refuse to join his friends, or on some sudden plea abruptly quit their society. And he still more unaccountably, and as it seemed systematically, avoided meeting his pretty neighbour Nina, whose father occupied the next tenement to his own. At the age of seventeen, Nina was as charming a picture of youth, cheerfulness, innocence, and confidence, as you could have seen in all the world. You could not look into her limpid eyes, which steadily returned your gaze, without seeing to the bottom of the pure and transparent spring of her thoughts. Why, then, did Arnod shrink from meeting her? He was young; had a little property; had health and industry; and he had told his friends he had formed no ties in other lands. Why, then, did he avoid the fascination of the pretty Nina, who seemed a being made to chase from any brow the clouds of gathering care? But he did so; yet less and less resolutely, for he felt the charm of her presence. Who could have done otherwise? And how could he long resist—he didn't—the impulse of his fondness for the innocent girl who often sought to cheer his fits of depression?

And they were to be united—were betrothed; yet still an anxious gloom would fitfully overcast his countenance, even in the sunshine of those hours.

"What is it, dear Arnod, that makes you sad? It cannot be on my account, I know, for you were sad before you ever noticed me; and that, I think," (and you should have seen the deepening rose upon her cheeks,) "surely first made me notice you."

"Nina," he answered, "I have done, I fear, a great

wrong in trying to gain your affections. Nina, I have a fixed impression that I shall not live; yet, knowing this, I have selfishly made my existence necessary to your happiness."

"How strangely you talk, dear Arnod! Who in the village is stronger and healthier than you? You feared no danger when you were a soldier. What danger do you fear as a villager of Meduegna?"

"It haunts me, Nina."

"But, Arnod, you were sad before you thought of me. Did you then fear to die?"

"Ah, Nina, it is something worse than death." And his vigorous frame shook with agony.

"Arnod, I conjure you, tell me."

"It was in Cossova this fate befell me. Here you have hitherto escaped the terrible scourge. But there they died, and the dead visited the living. I experienced the first frightful visitation, and I fled; but not till I had sought his grave, and exacted the dread expiation from the Vampyr."

Nina's blood ran cold. She stood horror-stricken. But her young heart soon mastered her first despair. With a touching voice she spoke—

"Fear not, dear Arnod; fear not now. I will be your shield, or I will die with you!"

And she encircled his neck with her gentle arms, and returning hope shone, Iris-like, amid her falling tears. Afterwards they found a reasonable ground for banishing or allaying their apprehension in the length of time which had elapsed since Arnod left Cossova, during which no fearful visitant had again approached him; and they fondly trusted *that* gave them security.

It is a strange world. The ills we fear are commonly not those which overwhelm us. The blows that reach us are for the most part unforeseen. One day, about a week after this conversation, Arnod missed his footing when on the top of a loaded hay-wagon, and fell from it to the ground. He was picked up insensible, and carried home, where, after lingering a short time, he died. His interment, as usual, followed immediately. His fate was sad and premature. But what pencil could paint Nina's grief!

Twenty or thirty days after his decease, says the perfectly authenticated report of these transactions, several of the neighbourhood complained that they were haunted by the deceased Arnod; and, what was more to the purpose, four of them died. The evil, looked at skeptically, was bad enough, but aggravated by the suggestions of superstition, it spread a panic through the whole district. To allay the popular terror, and if possible to get at the root of the evil, a determination was come to publicly to disinter the body of Arnod, with the view of ascertaining whether he really was a Vampyr, and, in that event, of treating him conformably. The day fixed for this proceeding was the fortieth after his burial.

It was on a gray morning in early August that the commission visited the quiet cemetery of Meduegna, which, surrounded with a wall of unhewn stone, lies sheltered by the mountain that, rising in undulating green slopes, irregularly planted with fruit trees, ends in an abrupt craggy ridge, feathered with underwood. The graves were, for the most part, neatly kept, with borders of box, or something like it, and flowers between; and at the head of most a small wooden cross, painted black, bearing the name of the tenant. Here and there a stone had been raised. One of considerable height, a single narrow slab, ornamented with grotesque Gothic carvings, dominated over the rest. Near this lay the grave of Arnod Paole, towards which the party moved. The work of throwing out the earth was begun by the gray, crooked old sexton, who lived in the Leichenhaus, beyond the great crucifix. He seemed unconcerned enough; no Vampyr would think of extracting a supper out of him. Nearest the grave stood two military surgeons, or feldscherers, from Belgrade, and a drummer-boy, who held their case of instruments. The boy looked on with keen interest; and when the coffin was exposed and rather roughly drawn out of the grave, his pale face and bright intent eye showed how the scene moved him. The sexton lifted the lid of the coffin: the body had become inclined to one side. Then turning it straight, "Ha! ha!" said he, pointing to fresh blood upon the lips—"Ha! ha! What! Your mouth not wiped since last night's work?" The spectators shuddered; the drummer-boy sank forward, fainting, and upset the instrument-case, scattering its contents; the senior surgeon, infected with the horror of the scene, repressed a hasty exclamation, and simply crossed himself. They threw water on the drummer-boy, and he recovered, but would not leave the spot. Then they inspected the body of Arnod. It looked as if it had not been dead a day. On handling it, the scarf-skin came off, but below were *new skin and new nails!* How could *they* have come there but from its foul feeding! The case was clear enough; there lay before them the thing they dreaded—the Vampyr. So, without more ado, they simply drove a stake through poor Arnod's chest, whereupon a quantity of blood gushed forth, and the corpse uttered an audible groan. "Murder! oh, murder!" shrieked the drummer-boy, as he rushed wildly, with convulsed gestures, from the cemetery.

The drummer-boy was not far from the mark. But, quitting the romancing vein, which had led me to try and restore the original colours of the picture, let me confine myself, in describing the rest of the scene and what followed, to the words of my authority.

The body of Arnod was then burnt to ashes, which were returned to the grave. The authorities further staked and burnt the bodies of the four others which were supposed to have been infected by Arnod. No mention is made of the state in which they were found. The adoption of these decisive measures failed, however, entirely to extinguish the evil, which continued still to hang about the village. About five years afterwards it had again become very rife, and many died through it; whereupon the authorities determined to make another and a complete clearance of the Vampyrs in the cemetery, and with that object they had all the graves, to which present suspicion attached, opened, and their contents officially anatomized, of which procedure the following is the medical report, here and there *abridged* only:—

1. A woman of the name of Stana, twenty years of age, who had died three months before of a three days' illness following her confinement. She had before her death avowed that she had *anointed* herself with the blood of a Vampyr, to liberate herself from his persecution. Nevertheless, she, as well as her infant, whose body through careless interment had been half eaten by the

dogs, had died. Her body was entirely free from decomposition. On opening it, the chest was found full of recently effused blood, and the bowels had exactly the appearances of sound health. The skin and nails of her hands and feet were loose and came off, but underneath lay new skin and nails.

2. A woman of the name of Miliza, who had died at the end of a three months' illness. The body had been buried ninety and odd days. In the chest was liquid blood. The viscera were as in the former instance. The body was declared by a heyduk, who recognised it, to be in better condition, and fatter, than it had been in the woman's legitimate lifetime.

3. The body of a child eight years old, that had likewise been buried ninety days: it was in the Vampyr condition.

4. The son of a heyduk named Milloc, sixteen years old. The body had lain in the grave nine weeks. He had died after three days' indisposition, and was in the condition of a Vampyr.

5. Joachim, likewise son of a heyduk, seventeen years old. He had died after three days' illness; had been buried eight weeks and some days; was found in the Vampyr state.

6. A woman of the name of Rusha, who had died of an illness of ten days' duration, and had been six weeks buried, in whom likewise fresh blood was found in the chest.

(The reader will understand, that to *see* blood in the chest, it is first necessary to *cut* the chest open.)

7. The body of a girl of ten years of age, who had died two months before. It was likewise in the Vampyr state, perfectly undecomposed, with blood in the chest.

8. The body of the wife of one Hadnuck, buried seven weeks before; and that of her infant, eight weeks old, buried only twenty-one days. They were both in a state of decomposition, though buried in the same ground, and closely adjoining the others.

9. A servant, by name Rhade, twenty-three years of age; he had died after an illness of three months' duration, and the body had been buried five weeks. It was in a state of decomposition.

10. The body of the heyduk Stanco, sixty years of age, who had died six weeks previously. There was much blood and other fluid in the chest and abdomen, and the body was in the Vampyr condition.

11. Millac, a heyduk, twenty-five years old. The body had been in the earth six weeks. It was perfectly in the Vampyr condition.

12. Stanjoika, the wife of a heyduk, twenty years old; had died after an illness of three days, and had been buried eighteen. The countenance was florid. There was blood in the chest and in the heart. The viscera were perfectly sound; the skin remarkably fresh.

The document which gives the above particulars is signed by three regimental surgeons, and formally countersigned by a lieutenant-colonel and sub-lieutenant. It bears the date of "June 7, 1732, Meduegna near Belgrade." No doubt can be entertained of its authenticity, or of its *general* fidelity; the less that it does not stand alone, but is supported by a mass of evidence to the same effect. It appears to establish, beyond question, that where the fear of Vampyrism prevails, and there occur several deaths, in the popular belief connected with it, the bodies, when disinterred weeks after burial, present the appearance of corpses from which life has only recently departed.

What inference shall we draw from this fact?—that Vampyrism is true in the popular sense?—and that these fresh-looking and well-conditioned corpses had some mysterious source of preternatural nourishment? That would be to adopt, not to solve the superstition. Let us content ourselves with a notion not so monstrous, but still startling enough: that the bodies, which were found in the so-called Vampyr state, instead of being in a new or mystical condition, were simply alive in the common way, or had been so for some time subsequent to their interment; that, in short, they were the bodies of persons who had been buried alive, and whose life, where it yet lingered, was finally extinguished through the ignorance and barbarity of those who disinterred them. In the following sketch of a similar scene to that above described, the correctness of this inference comes out with terrific force.

Erasmus Francisci, in his remarks upon the description of the Dukedom of Krain by Valvasor, speaks of a man of the name of Grando, in the district of Kring, who died, was buried, and became a Vampyr, and as such was exhumed for the purpose of having a stake thrust through him.

"When they opened his grave, after he had been long buried, his face was found with a colour, and his features made natural sorts of movements, as if the dead man smiled. He even opened his mouth as if he would inhale fresh air. They held the crucifix before him, and called in a loud voice, 'See, this is Jesus Christ who redeemed your soul from hell, and died for you.' After the sound had acted on his organs of hearing, and he had connected perhaps some ideas with it, tears began to flow from the dead man's eyes. Finally, when after a short prayer for his poor soul, they proceeded to hack off his head, the corpse uttered a screech, and turned and rolled just as if it had been alive—and the grave was full of blood."

We have thus succeeded in interpreting one of the unknown terms in the Vampyr theorem. The suspicious character, who had some dark way of nourishing himself in the grave, turns out to be an unfortunate gentleman (or lady) whom his friends had buried under a mistake while he was still alive, and who, if they afterwards mercifully let him alone, died sooner or later either naturally or of the premature interment—in either case, it is to be hoped, with no interval of restored consciousness. The state which thus passed for death and led to such fatal consequences, apart from superstition, deserves our serious consideration; for, although of very rare, it is of continual occurrence, and society is not sufficiently on its guard against a contingency so dreadful when overlooked. When the nurse or the doctor has announced that all is over—that the valued friend or relative has breathed his last—no doubt crosses any one's mind of the reality of the sad event. Disease is now so well understood—every step in its march laid down and foreseen—the approach of danger accurately estimated—the liability of the patient, according to his powers of resisting it, to succumb earlier or to hold out longer—all is theoretically so clear that a wholesome suspicion of error in the verdict of the attendants seldom suggests itself. The evil I am considering ought not, however, to be attributed to redundance of knowledge: it arises from its partial lack—from a too general neglect of one very important section in pathological science. The laity, if not the doctors too, constantly lose sight of the fact, that there exists an alternative to the fatal event of ordinary disease; that a patient is liable at any period of illness to deviate, or, as it were, to slide off, from the customary line of disease into another and a deceptive route—*instead of death, to encounter apparent death.*

The Germans express this condition of the living body by the term "scheintod," which signifies exactly *apparent death;* and it is perhaps a better term than our English equivalent, "suspended animation." But both these expressions are generic terms, and a specific term is still wanted to denote the present class of instances. To meet this exigency, I propose, for reasons which will afterwards appear, to employ the term "death-trance" to designate the cases we are investigating.

Death-trance is, then, one of the forms of suspended animation: there are several others. After incomplete poisoning, after suffocation in either of its various ways, after exposure to cold in infants newly born, a state is occasionally met with, of which (however each may still differ from the rest) the common feature is an apparent suspension of the vital actions. But all of these so-cited instances agree in another important respect, which second inter-agreement separates them as a class from death-trance. They represent, each and all, a period of conflict between the effects of certain deleterious impressions and the vital principle, the latter struggling against the weight and force of the former. Such is not the case in death-trance.

Death-trance is a positive status—a period of repose

—the duration of which is sometimes definite and predetermined, though unknown. Thus the patient, the term of the death-trance having expired, occasionally suddenly wakes, entirely and at once restored. Oftener, however, the machinery which has been stopped seems to require to be jogged—then it goes on again.

The basis of death-trance is suspension of the action of the heart, and of the breathing, and of voluntary motion; generally likewise feeling and intelligence, and the vegetative changes in the body, are suspended. With these phenomena is joined loss of external warmth; so that the usual evidence of life is gone. But there have occurred varieties of this condition, in which occasional slight manifestations of one or other of the vital actions have been observed.

Death-trance may occur as a primary affection, suddenly or gradually. The diseases the course of which it is liable, as it were, to bifurcate, or to graft itself upon, are first and principally all disorders of the nervous system. But in any form of disease, when the body is brought to a certain degree of debility, death-trance may supervene. Age and sex have to do with its occurrence; which is more frequent in the young than in the old, in women than in men—differences evidently connected with greater irritability of the nervous system. Accordingly, women in labour are among the most liable to death-trance, and it is from such a case that I will give a first instance of the affection as portrayed by a medical witness. (*Journal des Savans*, 1749.)

M. Rigaudeaux, surgeon to the military hospital, and licensed accoucher at Douai, was sent for on the 8th of September, 1745, to attend the wife of Francis Dumont, residing two leagues from the town. He was late in getting there; it was half-past eight, A. M.—too late, it seemed; the patient was declared to have died at six o'clock, after eighteen hours of ineffectual labour-pains. M. Rigaudeaux inspected the body; there was no pulse or breath; the mouth was full of froth, the abdomen tumid. He brought away the infant, which he committed to the care of the nurses, who, after trying to reanimate it for three hours, gave up the attempt, and prepared to lay it out, when it opened its mouth. They then gave it wine, and it was speedily recovered. M. Rigaudeaux, who returned to the house as this occurred, inspected again the body of the mother. (It had been already nailed down in a coffin.) He examined it with the utmost care; but he came to the conclusion that it was certainly dead. Nevertheless, as the joints of the limbs were still flexible, although seven hours had elapsed since its apparent death, he left the strictest injunctions to watch the body carefully, to apply stimulants to the nostrils from time to time, to slap the palms of the hands, and the like. At half-past three o'clock symptoms of returning animation showed themselves, and the patient recovered.

The period during which every ordinary sign of life may be absent, without the prevention of their return, is unknown, but in well-authenticated cases it has much exceeded the period observed in the above instance. Here is an example borrowed from the *Journal des Savans*, 1741.

There was a Colonel Russell, whose wife, to whom he was affectionately attached, died, or appeared to do so. But he would not allow the body to be buried; and threatened to shoot any one who should interfere to remove it for that purpose. His conduct was guided by reason as well as by affection and instinct. He said he would not part from the body till its decomposition had begun. Eight days had passed, during which the body of his wife gave no sign of life: when, as he sat bedewing her hand with his tears, the church-bell tolled, and, to his unspeakable amazement, his wife sat up and said—"That is the last bell; we shall be too late." She recovered.

There are cases on record of persons, who could spontaneously fall into death-trance. Monti, in a letter to Haller, adverts to several; and mentions, in particular, a peasant upon whom, when he assumed this state, the flies would settle; breathing, the pulse, and all ordinary signs of life disappeared. A priest of the name of Cælius Rhodaginus had the same faculty. But the most celebrated instance is that of Colonel Townshend, mentioned in the surgical works of Gooch, by whom and by Dr. Cheyne and Dr. Baynard, and by Mr. Shrine, an apothecary, the performance of Colonel Townshend was seen and attested. They had long attended him, for he was an habitual invalid, and he had often invited them to witness the phenomenon of his dying and coming to life again; but they had hitherto refused, from fear of the consequences to himself: at last they assented. Accordingly, in their presence, Colonel Townshend laid himself down on his back, and Dr. Cheyne undertook to observe his pulse; Dr. Baynard laid his hand on his heart, and Mr. Shrine had a looking-glass to hold to his mouth. After a few seconds, pulse, breathing, and the action of the heart, were no longer to be observed. Each of the witnesses satisfied himself of the entire cessation of these phenomena. When the death-trance had lasted half-an-hour, the doctors began to fear that their patient had pushed the experiment too far, and was dead in earnest; and they were preparing to leave the house, when a slight movement of the body attracted their attention. They renewed their routine of observation; when the pulse and sensible motion of the heart gradually returned, and breathing, and consciousness. The tale ends abruptly. Colonel Townshend, on recovering, sent for his attorney, made his will, and died, for good and all, six hours afterwards.

Although many have recovered from death-trance, and there seems to be in each case a definite period to its duration, yet its event is not always so fortunate. The patient sometimes really dies during its continuance, either unavoidably, or in consequence of adequate measures not being taken to stimulate him to waken, or to support life. The following very good instance rests on the authority of Dr. Schmidt, a physician of the hospital of Paderborn, where it occurred, (*Rheinisch-Westphälischer Anzeiger*, 1835, No. 57 and 58.)

A young man of the name of Caspar Kreite, from Berne, died in the hospital of Paderborn, but his body could not be interred for three weeks, for the following reasons. During the first twenty-four hours after drawing its last breath, the corpse opened its eyes, and the pulse could be felt, for a few minutes, beating feebly and irregularly. On the third and fourth day, points of the skin, which had been burned to test the reality of his death, suppurated. On the fifth day the corpse changed the position of one hand: on the ninth day a vesicular eruption appeared on the back. For nine days there was a vertical fold of the skin of the forehead—a sort of frown—and the features had not the character of death. The lips remained red till the eighteenth day; and the joints preserved their flexibility from first to last. He lay in this state in a warm room for nineteen days, without any farther alteration than a sensible wasting in flesh. Till after the nineteenth day no discoloration of the body, or odour of putrefaction, was observed. He had been cured of ague, and laboured under a slight chest affection; but there had been no adequate cause for his death. It is evident that this person was much more alive than many are in the death-trance; and one half suspects that stimulants and nourishment, properly introduced, might have entirely reanimated him.

I might exemplify death-trance by many a well authenticated romantic story. A noise heard in a vault; the people, instead of breaking open the door, go for the keys, and for authority to act, and return too late; the unfortunate person is found dead, having previously gnawn her hand and arm in agony.—A lady is buried with a jewel of value on her finger; thieves open the vault to possess themselves of the treasure; the ring cannot be drawn from the finger, and the thieves proceed to cut the finger off; the lady, wakening from her trance, scares the thieves away, and recovers.—A young married lady dies and is buried; a former admirer, to whom her parents had refused her hand, bribes the sexton to let him see once more the form he loved. The body opportunely comes to life at this moment, and flies from Paris with its first lover to England, where they are married. Venturing to return to France, the lady is recognised, and is reclaimed by her previous husband through a suit at law; her counsel demurs, on the ground of the desertion and burial; but the law not admitting this plea, she flies again to England with her preserver, to avoid the judgment of the parliament of Paris, in the acts of which the case stands recorded. There are one or two other cases that I dare not cite, the particulars of which transcend the wildest flights of imagination.

It may be thought that these are all tales of the olden time; and that the very case I have given from the hospital at Paderborn shows that now medical men are sufficiently circumspect, and the public really on its guard to prevent a living person being interred as one dead. And I grant that in England, among all but the poorest class, the danger is practically inconsiderable of being buried alive. But that it still exists for every class, and that for the poor the danger is great and serious, I am afraid there is too much reason for believing. It is stated in Froriep's *Notizen*, 1829, No. 522, that, agreeably to a then recent ordinance in New York, coffins presented for burial were kept above ground eight days, open at the head, and so arranged, that the least movement of the body would ring a bell, through strings attached to the hands and feet. It will hardly be credited, that *out of twelve hundred* whose interment had been thus postponed, *six returned to life*—one in every two hundred! The arrangement thus beneficently adopted at New York is, however, imperfect, as it makes time the criterion for interment. The time is *not* known during which a body in death-trance may remain alive. Nothing but one positive condition of the body, which I will presently mention, authenticates death. It is frightful to think how, in the south of Europe, within twenty-four hours after the last breath bodies are shovelled into pits among heaped corpses; and to imagine what fearful agonies of despair must sometimes be encountered by unhappy beings, who wake amid the unutterable horrors of such a grave. But it is enough to look at home, and to make no delay in providing there for the careful watching of the bodies of the poor, till life has certainly departed. Many do not dream how barbarous and backward the vaunted nineteenth century will appear to posterity!

But there is another danger to which society is obnoxious through not making sufficient account of the contingency of death-trance, that appears to me more urgent and menacing than even the risk of being buried alive.

The danger I advert to is not *this;* but this is something—

The Cardinal Espinosa, prime minister under Philip the Second of Spain, died, as it was supposed, after a short illness. His rank entitled him to be embalmed. Accordingly, the body was opened for that purpose. The lungs and heart had just been brought into view, when the latter was seen to beat. The cardinal awakening at the fatal moment, had still strength enough left to seize with his hand the knife of the anatomist!

But it is *this*—

On the 23d of September, 1763, the Abbé Prevost, the French novelist and compiler of travels, was seized with a fit in the forest of Chantilly. The body was found, and conveyed to the residence of the nearest clergyman. It was supposed that death had taken place through apoplexy. But the local authorities, desiring to be satisfied of the fact, ordered the body to be examined. During the process, the poor abbé uttered a cry of agony.—It was too late.

It is to be observed that cases of sudden and unexplained death are, on the one hand, the cases most likely to furnish a large percentage of death-trance; and, on the other, are just those in which the anxiety of friends or the over-zealousness of a coroner is liable to lead to premature anatomization. Nor does it even follow that, because the body happily did not wake while being dissected, the spark of life was therefore extinct. This view, however, is too painful to be followed out in reference to the past. But it imperatively suggests the necessity of forbidding necroscopic examinations, before there is perfect evidence that life has departed—that is, of extending to this practice the rule which ought to be made absolute in reference to interment.

Thus comes out the practical importance of the question, how is it to be known that the body is no longer alive?

The entire absence of the ordinary signs of life is insufficient to prove the absence of life. The body may be externally cold; the pulse not be felt; breathing may have ceased; no bodily motion may occur; the limbs may be stiff (through spasm;) the sphincter muscles relaxed; no blood may flow from an opened vein; the eyes may have become glassy; there may be partial *mortification* to offend the sense with the smell of death; and yet the body may be alive.

The only security we at *present* know of, that life has left the body, is the supervention of chemical decomposition, shown in commencing change of colour of the integuments of the abdomen and throat to blue and green, and an attendant cadaverous fetor.

To return from this important digression to the former subject of the Vampyr superstition. The second element which we have yet to explain is the Vampyr visit and its consequence—the lapse of the party visited into death-trance. There are two ways of dealing with this knot; one is to cut it, the other to untie it.

It may be cut, by denying the supposed connexion between the Vampyr visit and the supervention of death-trance in the second party. Nor is the explanation thus obtained devoid of plausibility. There is no reason why death-trance should not, in certain seasons and places, be *epidemic*. Then the persons most liable to it would be those of weak and irritable nervous systems. Again, a first effect of the epidemic might be further to shake the nerves of weaker subjects. These are exactly the persons who are likely to be infected with imaginary terrors, and to dream, or even to fancy, they have seen Mr. or Mrs. such a one, the last victims of the epidemic. The dream or impression upon the senses might again recur, and the sickening patient have already talked of it to his neighbours, before he himself was seized with death-trance. On this supposition, the Vampyr visit would sink into the subordinate rank of a mere premonitory symptom.

To myself, I must confess, this explanation, the best I am yet in a position to offer, appears barren and jejune; and not at all to do justice to the force and frequency, or, as tradition represents the matter, the universality of the Vampyr visit as a precursor of the victim's fate. Imagine how strong must have been the conviction of the reality of the apparition, how common a feature it must have been, to have led to the laying down of the unnatural and repulsive process customarily followed at the Vampyr's grave, as the regular and proper preventive of ulterior consequences.

I am disposed, therefore, rather to try and untie this knot, and with that object to wait, hoping that something may turn up in the progress of these inquiries to assist me in its solution. In the mean time, I would beg leave to consider this second half of the problem a compound phenomenon, the solutions of the two parts of which may not emerge simultaneously. The Vampyr visit is one thing; its presumed contagious effect another.

The Vampyr visit! Well, it is clear the Vampyr could not have left his grave bodily—or, at all events, if he could, he never could have buried himself again. Yet in his grave they always found him. So the body could not have been the visitant. Then, in popular language, it was the ghost of the Vampyr that haunted its future victim. The ghostly nature of the visitant could not have been identified at a luckier moment. The very subject which I next propose to undertake is the analysis of ghosts. I have, therefore, only to throw the Vampyr ghost into the crucible with the rest; and to-morrow I may perhaps be able to report the rational composition of the whole batch.

LETTER III.

Unreal Ghosts—Law of Sensorial Illusions—Cases of Nicolai, Schwedenborg, Joan of Arc—Fetches—Churchyard ghosts.

The projected analysis has been crowned with success. The fumes of superstition have been driven off, and the ghosts have been reduced to rational elements. All trace of supernatural agency has vanished; and in its place are found three principles—one physical, two psychical—by the help of which every conceivable ghost may in future be alternately decomposed and recompounded by the merest tyro.

The first of which I shall describe the nature and operation is a psychical truth, already known to most persons of education. It is of very general use in ghost-building; it forms the immediate *personnel* of every ghost; and is of so active a nature that alone, or assisted by a little credulity, it is enough to constitute the simplest kind—a common fetch. Mixed with a dose of mental anxiety, or as much remorse as will lie on the point of a dagger, it will form a troublesome retrospective ghost. The second principle—a physical one, less generally known—is the basis of that sturdy apparition the churchyard ghost, which it will turn out in very fair style aided by fancy alone; but, to perfect the illusive result, the co-operation of the first principle is necessary. The third, an entirely new one, is the foundation of real ghosts—that is, of ghosts which announce unexpected events, distant in space or time; the same principle is concerned in true dreams, and in second-sight.

The first of the three principles adverted to is the physiological fact that, when the blood is heated, the nervous system overstrained, or digestion out of sorts, the thereby directly or sympathetically disordered brain is liable to project before us illusory forms, which are coloured and move like life, and are so far undistinguishable from reality. Sometimes a second sense is drawn into the phantasmagoria, and the fictitious beings speak as you do. Almost always the illusion stops there. But in one or two marvellous cases, the touch has been involved in the hallucination, and the ghost has been tangible. These phenomena are termed sensorial illusions. The visual part of them, the first and commonest, has been the most attended to. The cause immediately producing it appears to be an affection, not of the organ of vision, but of that part of the brain in which the nerves of seeing take their origin. This organ it is which in health realizes our sensations of colour, and converts them into visual perceptions. Like other parts of the brain, it is stored with memories of its past impressions, ready to be evoked—either pure and true by conception, or any how combined by fancy. In perfect health, a chance moment of warm recollection will call up from this source the once familiar face transiently, but how distinctly!

In its morbid state, the beings it projects before us are for the most part strangers, just as the personages we meet in our dreams are exceptionally only our living and present acquaintance.

The most instructive case of sensorial illusions on record, as containing the largest illustration of the phenomena, is that of Nicolai, the bookseller of Berlin.

The narrative was read before the Academy of Sciences at Berlin, in 1799. Its substance runs thus:—Nicolai had met with some family troubles, which much disturbed him. Then, on the first of January, 1791, there stood before him, at the distance of ten paces, the ghost of his eldest son. He pointed at it, directing his wife to look. She saw it not, and tried to convince Nicolai that it was an illusion. In a quarter of an hour it vanished. In the afternoon, at four o'clock, it came again. Nicolai was alone. He went to his wife's room, the ghost followed him. About six other apparitions joined the first, and they walked about among each other. After some days the apparition of his son stayed away; but its place was filled with the figures of a number of persons, some known, some unknown to Nicolai—some of dead, others of living persons. The known ones represented distant acquaintances only. The figures of none of Nicolai's habitual friends were there. The appearances were almost always human; occasionally a man on horseback, and birds, and dogs, would present themselves. The apparitions came mostly after dinner, at the commencement of digestion; they were just like real persons, the colouring a thought fainter. The apparitions were equally distinct whether Nicolai was alone or in society, in the dark as by day; in his own house or in those of others; but in the latter case they were less frequent, and they very seldom made their appearance in the streets. During the first eight days they seemed to take very little notice of one another, but walked about like people at a fair, only here and there communing with each other. They took no notice of Nicolai, or of the remarks he addressed regarding them to his wife and physician. No effort of his would dismiss them, or bring an absent one back. When he shut his eyes, they sometimes disappeared, sometimes remained; when he opened his eyes, they were there as before. After a week they became more numerous, and began to converse. They conversed with one another first, and then addressed him. Their remarks were short and unconnected, but sensible and civil. His acquaintances inquired after his health, and expressed sympathy with him, and spoke in terms comforting him. The apparitions were most conversable when he was alone; nevertheless, they mingled in the conversation when others were by, and their voices had the same sound as those of real persons. The illusion went on thus from the 24th of February to the 20th of April; so that Nicolai, who was in good bodily health, had time to become tranquillized about the nature of his visiters, and to observe them at his ease. At last they rather amused him; then the doctors thought of an efficient plan of treatment. They prescribed leeches; and then followed the "denouement" of this interesting representation. The apparitions became pale, and vanished. On the 20th of April, at the time of applying the leeches, Nicolai's room was full of figures moving about among each other. They first began to have a less lively motion; shortly afterwards their colours became paler, in another half hour paler still, though the forms still remained. About seven o'clock in the evening the figures had become colourless, and they moved scarcely at all; but their outline was still tolerably perfect. Gradually that became less and less defined; at last they disappeared, breaking into air, fragments only remaining, which at last all vanished. By eight o'clock all were gone, and Nicolai subsequently saw no more of them.

In general, as in Nicolai's case, the sight is the sense at first and alone affected. Illusions of the hearing, if they occur, follow later. In some most extraordinary cases, I have observed that the touch has likewise participated in the affection; the following is an instance:—

Herr von Baczko, already subject to visual hallucinations of a diseased nervous system, his right side weak with palsy, his right eye blind, and the vision of the left imperfect, was engaged one evening shortly after the battle of Jena, as he tells in his autobiography, in translating a pamphlet into Polish, when he felt a poke in his loins. He looked round, and found that it proceeded from a Negro or Egyptian boy, seemingly about twelve years of age. Although he was persuaded the whole was an illusion, he thought it best to knock the apparition down, when he felt that it offered a sensible resistance. The Negro then attacked him on the other side, and gave his left arm a particularly disagreeable twist, when Baczko again pushed him off. The Negro continued to visit him constantly during four months, preserving the same appearance, and remaining tangible; then he came seldomer; and, finally appearing as a brown-coloured apparition with an owl's head, he took his leave.

Sensorial illusions, technically speaking, are not mental delusions; or they become so only when they are believed to be realities. So sensorial illusions are not insanity, neither do they menace that disorder: they are not its customary precursors. Nevertheless, they may accompany the first outbreak of madness; and they occur much more frequently in lunatics than in persons of sound mind. In insanity they are firmly believed in by the patient, whose delusions they may either suggest or be shaped by.

In insanity, illusions of the hearing often occur alone, which is comparatively rare in sane people.

The objects of visual illusions are commonly men and women; but animals, and even inanimate objects, sometimes constitute them. A lady whose sight was failing her had long visions every day of rows of buildings, houses, and parks, and such like. The subjects of visual illusions are generally perfectly trivial, like the events of a common dream. But, though susceptible of change, their custom is to recur with much the same character daily. One patient could at will summon the apparition of an acquaintance to join the rest; but, once there, he could not get rid of him.

Sometimes it happens that sensorial illusions are in accordance with a congenial train of thought—for instance, with peculiar impressions referring to religion. They are then very liable to be construed by the patient into realities, and to materially influence his conversation and conduct. He remains, no doubt, strictly sane in the midst of these delusions. But he is apt not to be thought so; or, to use a figure, the world's opinion of such a person becomes a polar force, and society is divided into his admiring followers and those who think him a lunatic. Such was, and remains, the fate of Schwedenborg.

Schwedenborg, the son of a Swedish clergyman of the name of Schwedberg, ennobled as Schwedenborg, was up to the year 1743, which was the fifty-fourth of his age, an ordinary man of the world, distinguished only in literature, having written many volumes on philosophy and science, and being professor in the Mineralogical School, where he was much respected. On a sudden, in the year 1743, he believed himself to have got into a commerce with the world of spirits, which so fully took possession of his thoughts, that he not only published their revelations, but was in the habit of detailing their daily chat with him. Thus he says, "I had a conversation the other day on that very point with the apostle Paul," or with Luther, or some other dead person. Schwedenborg continued in what he believed to be constant communion with spirits till his death, in 1772. He was, without doubt, in the fullest degree convinced of the reality of his spiritual commerce. So in a letter to the Wurtemburg Prelate, Oetinger, dated November 11, 1766, he uses the following words: "If I have spoken with the apostles? To this I answer, I conversed with St. Paul during a whole year, particularly with reference to the text, Romans iii. 28. I have three times conversed with St. John, once with Moses, and a hundred times with Luther, who allowed that it was against the warning of an angel that he professed *fidem solam*, and that he stood alone upon the separation from the Pope. With angels, finally, have I these twenty years conversed, and converse daily."

Of the angels, he says, "They have human forms, the appearance of men, as I have a thousand times seen; for I have spoken with them as a man with other men—often with several together—and I have seen nothing in the least to distinguish them from other men." They had, in fact, exactly the same appearance as Nicolai's visiters. "Lest any one should call this an illusion, or imaginary perception, it is to be understood that I am accustomed to see them when myself perfectly wide awake, and in full exercise of my observation. The speech of an angel, or of a spirit, sounds like and as loud as that of a man; but it is not heard by the bystanders. The reason is, that *the speech of an angel, or a spirit, finds entrance first into a man's thoughts, and reaches his organs of hearing from within.*" A wonderful instance this last reason how it is possible *cum ratione insanire;* he analyzes the illusion perfectly, even when he is most deceived by it.

"The angels who converse with men speak not in their own language, but in the language of the country; and likewise in other languages which are known to a man, not in languages which he does not understand." Schwedenborg here interrupted the angels, and, to explain the matter, observed that they most likely appeared to speak his mother tongue, *because, in fact,* it was not they who spoke, but himself after their suggestions. The angels would not allow this, and went away at the close of the conversation unpersuaded.

The following fiction is very fine: "When approaching, the angels often appear like a ball of light; and they travel in companies so grouped together—they are allowed so to unite by the Lord—that they may act as one being, and share each other's ideas and knowledge; and in this form they bound through the universe, from planet to planet."

A still more interesting example of the influence of sensorial illusions on human conduct is furnished by the touching history of Joan of Arc.

"It is now seven years ago," so spoke before her judges the simple but high-minded maiden—"it was a summer day, towards the middle hour, I was about thirteen years old, and was in my father's garden, that I heard for the first time, on my right hand, towards the church, a voice, and there stood a figure in a bright radiance before my eyes. It had the appearance and look of a right good and virtuous man, bore wings, was surrounded with light on all sides, and by the angels of heaven. It was the archangel Michael. The voice seemed to me to command respect; but I was yet a child, and was frightened at the figure, and doubted very much whether it were the archangel. I saw him and the angels as distinctly before my eyes as I now see you, my judges." With words of encouragement the archangel announced to her that God had taken pity upon France, and that she must hasten to the assistance of the King. At the same time he promised her that St. Catharine and St. Margaret would shortly visit her: he told her that she should do what they commanded her, because they were sent by God to guide and conduct her. "Upon this," continued Joan, "St. Catharine and St. Margaret appeared to me, as the archangel had foretold. They ordered me to get ready to go to Robert de Beaudricourt, the King's captain. He would several times refuse me, but at last would consent, and give me people who would conduct me to the King. Then should I raise the siege of Orleans. I replied to them that I was a poor child, who understood nothing about riding on horseback and making war. They said I should carry my banner with courage; God would help me, and win back for my king his entire kingdom. As soon as I knew," continued Joan, "that I was to proceed on this errand, I avoided as much as I could taking part in the sports and amusements of my young companions." "So have the saints conducted me during seven years, and have given me support and assistance in all my need and labours; and now at present," said she to her judges, "no day goes by but they come to see me." "I seldom see the saints that they are not surrounded with a halo of light; they wear rich and precious crowns, as it is reasonable they should. I see them always under the same forms, and have never found in their discourse any discrepancies. I know how to distinguish one from the other, and distinguish them as well by the sound of their voices as by their salutation. They come often without my calling upon them. But when they do not come, I pray to the Lord that he will send them to me; and never have I needed them but they have visited me."

Such is part of the defence of the heroic Joan of Arc, who was taken prisoner by the Duke of Burgundy on the 23d of May, 1430—sold by him for a large sum to the English, and by them put on her trial as a heretic, idolatress, and magician—condemned, and finally burned alive on the 30th of May, 1431!

Her innocence, simplicity, and courage incense one sadly against her judges; but it is likely there were at that time many good and sensible persons who approved of her sentence, and never suspected its cruelty and injustice. Making allowance for the ignorance and barbarity of the age, her treatment was, perhaps, not worse than that of Abd-el-Kader now. Her visions—they were palpably the productions of her own fancy, the figures of saints and angels, which she had seen in missals, projected before her mental sight; and their cause the instinctive workings, unknown to herself, of her young high-couraged and enthusiastic heart, shaping its suggestions into holy prophesyings—the leading facts of which her resolute will realized, while their actual discrepancies with subsequent events she pardonably forgot.*

I will present yet another and less pleasing picture, where the subject of sensorial illusions was of infirm mind, and they struck upon the insane chord, and reason jangled harshly out of tune. It would be a curious question whether such a sensorial illusion as overthrew the young

* I cannot deny that another principle, afterwards to be explained, may have been additionally in operation in this interesting case.

seer's judgment in the following case, could have occurred to a mind previously sane; whether, for instance, it could have occurred to Schwedenborg, and, in that event, how he would have dealt with it.

Arnold (a German writer) relates, in his history of the church and of heresy, how there was a young man in Königsberg, well educated, the natural son of a priest, who had the impression that he was met near a crucifix on the wayside by seven angels, who revealed to him that he was to represent God the Father on earth, to drive all evil out of the world, &c. The poor fellow, after pondering upon this illusion a long time, issued a circular, beginning thus:

"We John, Albrecht, Adelgreif, Syrdos, Amata, Kanemata, Kilkis, Mataldis, Schmalkilimundis, Sabrandis, Elioris, Hyperarch-High-priest and Emperor, Prince of Peace of the whole world, Hyperarch-King of the holy kingdom of Heaven, Judge of the living and of the dead, God and Father, in whose divinity Christ will come on the last day to judge the world, Lord of all lords, King of all kings," &c.

He was thereupon thrown into prison at Königsberg, where every means were used by the clergy to reclaim him from these blasphemous and heretical notions. To all their entreaties, however, he listened only with a smile of pity—"that they should think of reclaiming God the Father." He was then put to the torture, and as what he endured made no alteration in his convictions, he was condemned to have his tongue torn out with red-hot tongs, to be cut in four quarters, and then burned under the gallows. He wept bitterly, not at his own fate, but that they should pronounce such a sentence on the Deity. The executioner was touched with pity, and implored him to make a final recantation. But he persisted that he was God the Father, whether they pulled his tongue out by the roots or not; and so he was executed!

From the preceding forcible illustrations of the working of sensorial illusions on individual minds, it is to descend a little in interest to trace their ministry in giving rise to the rickety forms of popular superstition. However, the material may be the same, whether it be cast for the commemoration of a striking event or coined for vulgar currency. And here is a piece of the latter description, with the recommendation of being at least fresh from the mint, and spic-and-span new—an instance of superstition surviving in England in the middle of the nineteenth century.

A young gentleman, who has recently left Oxford, told me that he was one evening at a supper-party in college, when they were joined by a common friend on his return from hunting. They expected him, but were struck with his appearance. He was pale and agitated. On questioning him, they learned the cause. During the latter part of his ride home, he had been accompanied by a horseman, who kept exact pace with him, the rider and horse being close fac-similes of himself and the steed he rode, even to the copy of a new fangled bit which he sported that day for the first time. He had, in fact, seen his "double" or "Fetch," and it had shaken his nerves pretty considerably. His friends advised him to consult the college-tutor, who failed not to give him some good advice, and hoped the warning would not be thrown away. My informant, who thought the whole matter very serious, and was inclined to believe the unearthly visit to have been no idle one, added that it had made the ghost-seer, for the time at least, a wiser and better man.

Such a visionary duplicate of one's-self—one's fetch—is a not unfrequent form of sensorial illusion. In more ignorant days the appearance of a fetch excited much apprehension. It was supposed to menace death or serious calamity to its original. Properly viewed, unless it proceed from hard work and overstrained thought, (from which you can desist,) it indicates something wrong in your physical health, and its warning goes no further than to consult a doctor, to learn, "what rhubarb, senna, or what purgative drug will drive the spectre hence." The efficiency of such means was shown in the case of Nicolai. Yet in this case, I may remark, the originating cause of the attack had been anxiety about the very son whose apparition was the first of the throng to visit him. Had the illusion continued limited to the figure of the son, it would have been more questionable what art could do towards dismissing it. At all events, in such a case, the first thing is to remove the perilous stuff that weighs upon the mind. So the personage whose words I have been using was doubtless right, in his own case, to "throw physic to the dogs."

In the tragedy of *Macbeth*, sensorial illusions are made to play their part with curious physiological correctness. The mind of Macbeth is worn by the conflict between ambition and duty. At last his better resolves give way; and his excited fancy projects before him the fetch of his own dagger, which marshals him the way that he shall go. The spectator is thus artistically prepared for the further working of the same infirmity in the apparition of Banquo, which, unseen by his guests, is visible only to the conscience-stricken murderer. With a scientific precision no less admirable, the partner of his guilt—*a woman*—is made to have attacks of trance, (*to which women are more liable than men,*) caused by her disturbed mind; and in her trance the exact physiological character of one form of that disorder is portrayed—*she enacts a dream,* which is the essence of somnambulism.

One almost doubts whether Shakspeare was aware of the philosophic truth displayed in these master-strokes of his own art. The apparitions conjured up in the witch scenes of the same play, and the ghost in *Hamlet,* are moulded on the pattern of vulgar superstition. He employs indifferently the baser metal and the truthful inspirations of his own genius—realizing Shelley's strange figure of

> "a poet hidden
> In the light of thought."

So they say the sun is himself dark as a planet, and his atmosphere alone the source of light, through the gaps in which his common earth is seen. I am tempted—but it would be idle, and I refrain—to quote an expression or two, or a passage, from Shakspeare, exemplifying his wonderful turn for approximating to truths of which he must have been ignorant—where lines of admired and unaccountable beauty have unexpectedly acquired lucidity and appositeness through modern science. While, to make a quaint comparison, his great contemporary, Bacon, employed the lamp of his imagination to illuminate the paths to the discovery of truth, Shakspeare would, with random intuition, seize on the undiscovered truths themselves, and use them to vivify the conceptions of his fancy.

Let me now turn to explain a ghost of a more positive description—the churchyard ghost. The ghost will perhaps exclaim against so trivial a title, and one so unjust in reference to old superstition; but it will be seen he deserves no better. In popular story he had a higher office; his duty was to watch the body over which church rites had not been performed, that had been rudely inearthed after violent death. As thus—

There was a cottage in a village I could name to which a bad report attached. More than one who had slept in it had seen, at midnight, the radiant apparition of a little child standing on the hearth-stone. At length suspicion was awakened. The hearth-stone was raised, and there were found buried beneath it the remains of an infant. A story was now divulged how the last tenant and a female of the village had abruptly quitted the neighbourhood. The ghost was real and significant enough.

But here is a still better instance from a trustworthy German work, P. Kieffer's *Archives*. The narrative was communicated by Herr Ehrman of Strasburg, son-in-law of the well-known writer Pfeffel, from whom he received it.

The ghost-seer was a young candidate for orders, eighteen years of age, of the name of Billing. He was known to have very excitable nerves, had already experienced sensorial illusions, and was particularly sensitive to the presence of human remains, which made him tremble and shudder in all his limbs. Pfeffel, being blind, was accustomed to take the arm of this young man, and they walked thus together in Pfeffel's garden, near Colmar. At one spot in the garden, Pfeffel remarked that his companion's arm gave a sudden start, as if he had received an electric shock. Being asked what was the matter, Billing replied, "Nothing." But on their going over the same spot again, the same effect recurred. The young man being pressed to explain the cause of his disturbance, avowed that it arose from a peculiar sensation which he always experienced when in the vicinity of human remains; that it was his impression a human body must be interred there; but that, if Pfeffel would return with him at night, he should be able to speak with greater confidence. Accordingly they went together to the garden when it was dark, and as they approached the spot, Billing observed a faint light over it. At ten paces from it he stopped, and would go no farther, for he saw hovering over it, or self-supported in the air—its feet only a few inches from the ground—a luminous female figure, nearly five feet high, with the right arm folded on her breast, the left hanging by her side. When Pfeffel himself stepped forward and placed himself about where the figure appeared to be, Billing said it was now on his right hand, now on his left, now behind, now before him. When Pfeffel cut the air with his stick, it seemed as if it went through and divided a light flame, which then united again. The visit, repeated the next night, in company with some of Pfeffel's relatives, gave the same result. They did not see any thing. Pfeffel then, unknown to the ghost-seer, had the ground dug up, when there was found at some depth, beneath a layer of quicklime, a human body in progress of decomposition. The remains were removed, and the earth carefully replaced. Three days afterwards, Billing, from whom this whole proceeding had been kept concealed, was again led to the spot by Pfeffel. He walked over it now without experiencing any unusual impression whatever.

The explanation of this mysterious phenomenon has been but recently arrived at. The discoveries of Von Reichenbach, of which I gave a sketch in the first letter, announce the principle on which it depends. Among these discoveries is the fact that the Od force makes itself visible as a dim light or waving flame to highly sensitive subjects. Such persons, in the dark, see flames issuing from the poles of magnets and crystals. Von Reichenbach eventually discovered that the Od force is distributed universally, although in varying quantities. But among the causes which excite its evolution, one of the most active is chemical decomposition. Then, happening to remember Pfeffel's ghost story, it occurred to Von Reichenbach that what Billing had seen was possibly Od light. To test the soundness of this conjecture, Miss Reichel, a very sensitive subject, was taken at night to an extensive burying-ground near Vienna, where interments take place daily, and there are many thousand graves. The result did not disappoint Von Reichenbach's expectations. Whithersoever Miss Reichel turned her eyes, she saw masses of flame. This appearance manifested itself most about recent graves. About very old ones it was not visible. She described the appearance as resembling less bright flame than fiery vapour, something between fog and flame. In several instances the light extended four feet in height above the ground. When Miss Reichel placed her hand on it, it seemed to her involved in a cloud of fire. When she stood in it, it came up to her throat. She expressed no alarm, being accustomed to the appearance.

The mystery has thus been entirely solved; for it is evident that the spectral character of the luminous apparition, in the two instances which I have narrated, had been supplied by the seers themselves. So the superstition has vanished; but, as usual, it veiled a truth.

LETTER IV.

TRUE GHOSTS.—The apparitions themselves always sensorial illusions—The truth of their communications accounted for—Zschokke's Seer-gift described, to show the possibility of direct mental communication—Second-sight—The true relation of the mind to the living body.

THE worst of a true ghost is, that, to be sure of his genuineness—that is, of his veracity—one must wait the event. He is distinguished by no sensible and positive characteristics from the commoner herd. There is nothing in his outward appearance to raise him in your opinion above a fetch. But even this fact is not barren. His dress,—it is in the ordinary mode of the time, in nothing overdone. To be dressed thus does credit to his taste, as to be dressed at all evinces his sense of propriety; but alas! the same elements convict him of objective unreality. Whence come that aerial coat and waistcoat, whence those visionary trousers?—alas! they can only have issued from the wardrobe in the seer's fancy. And, like his dress, the wearer is imaginary, a mere sensorial illusion, without a shadow of externality; he is not more substantial than a dream.

But dreams have differences of quality no less than ghosts. All do not come through the ivory gate. Some are true and significant enough. See, there glides one skulking assassin-like into the shade,—he not long since killed his man; "Hilloa, ill-favoured Dream! come hither and give an account of yourself." (Enter Dream.)

A Scottish gentleman and his wife were travelling four or five years ago in Switzerland. There travelled with them a third party, an intimate friend, a lady, who some time before had been the object of a deep attachment on the part of a foreigner, a Frenchman. Well, she would have nothing to say to him on the topic uppermost in his mind, but she gave him a good deal of serious advice, which she probably thought he wanted; and she ultimately promoted, or was a cognizant party to, his union with a lady whom she likewise knew. The so-married couple were now in America; and the lady occasionally heard from them, and had every reason to believe they were both in perfect health. One morning, on their meeting at breakfast, she told her companions that she had had a very impressive dream the night before, which had recurred twice. The scene was a room in which lay a coffin; near to it stood her ex-lover in a luminous transfigured resplendent state; his wife was by, looking much as usual. The dream had caused the lady some misgivings, but her companions exhorted her to view it as a trick of her fancy, and she was half persuaded so to do. The dream, however, was right, notwithstanding. In process of time, letters arrived announcing the death, after a short illness, of the French gentleman, within the twenty-four hours in which the vision appeared. (Sensation—applause, followed by cries of Shame; the Dream, hurrying away, is hurt by the horn of the gate.)

It would be difficult to persuade the lady who dreamed this dream that there was no connexion between it and the event it foreshadowed in her mind beyond the accidental coincidence of time. Nevertheless, to this conclusion an indifferent auditor would probably come; and upon the following reasoning: We sometimes dream of the death of an absent friend when he is alive and in health, just as we sometimes dream that long-lost friends are alive. And it is quite possible—nay, likely to occur in the chapter of accidents—nay, certain to turn up now and then among the dreams of millions during centuries —that a fortuitous dream, seemingly referring to the fact, should be coincident in point of time with the death of a distant friend. To explain one such case, we need look no further than to the operation of chance. Why, then, ever seek another principle?

Let us examine a parallel ghost-story. A gentleman has a relative in India, healthy, of good constitution, in the civil service, prosperous: he has no cause for anxiety, and entertains none, respecting his relative. But one day he sees his ghost. In due course letters arrive mentioning the occurrence of his relative's death on that day. The case is more remarkable than the last; for the ghost-seer never in his life *but that once* experienced a sensorial illusion. Still, it is evidently possible that the two events were, through chance alone, coincident in time. And if in this case, why not in another?

Then let me adduce a more remarkable instance: A late General Wynyard, and the late General Sir John Sherbroke, when young men, were serving in Canada. One day—it was daylight—Mr. Wynyard and Mr. Sherbroke both saw pass through the room where they sat a figure, which Mr. Wynyard recognised as a brother then far away. One of the two walked to the door, and looked out upon the landing-place, but the stranger was not there; and a servant who was on the stairs had seen nobody pass out. In time news arrived that Mr. Wynyard's brother had died about the time of the visit of the apparition.

I have had opportunities of inquiring of two near relations of this General Wynyard upon what evidence the above story rests. They told me they had each heard it from his own mouth. More recently, a gentleman, whose accuracy of recollection exceeds that of most people, has told me that he had heard the late Sir John Sherbroke, the other party in the ghost-story, tell it much in the same way at a dinner-table.

One does not feel as comfortably satisfied that the complicated coincidences in this tale admit of being referred to chance. The odds are enormous against two persons —young men in perfect health, neither of whom before or after this event experienced a sensorial illusion—being the subjects at the same moment of one, their common and only one, which concurred in point of time with an event that it foreshadowed, unless there were some real connexion between the event and the double apparition. And we feel a nascent inclination to inquire whether— in case such instances as the present occasionally recur, and instances like the two before narrated become, when looked for, startingly multiplied—there exists any known mental or physical principle, by the help of which they may be explained into natural phenomena.

The more we look after facts of the above nature, the more urgent becomes the want of such a means of explanation. In every family circle, in every party of men accidentally brought together, you will be sure to hear, if the conversation fall on ghosts and dreams, one or more instances—which the narrators represent as well authenticated—of intimations of the deaths of absent persons conveyed to friends either through an apparition or a dream, or an equivalent unaccountable presentiment. A gentleman—himself of distinguished ability—told me that when he was an undergraduate at Cambridge, he was secretary to a ghost society formed in sportive earnest by some of the cleverest young men of one of the best modern periods of the university. One of the results of their labours was the collection of about a dozen stories of the above description resting upon good evidence.

Then there transpire occasionally cases with more curious features still. Not only is the general intimation of an event given, but minute particulars attending it are figured in the dream, or communicated by the ghost. Such tales have sometimes been authenticated in courts of justice. Here is one out of last week's newspaper:—

"In a Durham paper of last week, there was an account of the disappearance of Mr. Smith, gardener to Sir Clifford Constable, who, it was supposed, had fallen into the river Tees, his hat and stick having been found near the water-side. From that time up to Friday last the river had been dragged every day; but every effort so made to find the body proved ineffectual. On the night of Thursday, however, a person named Awde, residing at little Newsham, a small village about four miles from Wycliff, dreamt that Smith was laid under the ledge of a certain rock, about three hundred yards below Whorlton Bridge, and that *his right arm was broken.* Awde got up early on Friday, and his dream had such an effect upon him that he determined to go and search the river. He accordingly started off for that purpose, without mentioning the matter, being afraid that he would be laughed at by his neighbours. Nevertheless, on his arriving at the boat-house, he disclosed his object on the man asking him for what purpose he required the boat. He rowed to the spot he had seen in his dream; and there, strange to say, upon the very first trial that he made with his boat-hook, he pulled up the body of the unfortunate man, with his right arm actually broken."—(*Herald*, December, 1848.)

Reviewing all that I have advanced, it appears to me that there are two desiderata which pressingly require to be now supplied. First, some one should take the pains of authenticating at the time, and putting on permanent record, stories like the above, to be at the service of future speculators. But, secondly, so numerous and well attested are those already current, that the bringing forward into light of some principle by which they may be shown to be natural events is now peremptorily called for.

To lead to the supply of the second desideratum, I proceed to mention a physical phenomenon, which from time to time occurred to the late historian and novelist, Heinrich Zschokke. It is described by him in a sort of autobiography, entitled *Selbstschau*, which he published a few years ago. It was only last year that Zschokke died, having attained a good old age. Early brought into public life in the troubles of Switzerland, and afterwards maintaining his place in public consideration by his numerous writings, he was personally widely known: he was universally esteemed a man of strict veracity and integrity. He writes thus of himself:—

"If the reception of so many visiters was sometimes troublesome, it repaid itself occasionally either by making me acquainted with remarkable personages, or by bringing out a wonderful sort of seer-gift, which I called my inward vision, and which has always remained an enigma to me. I am almost afraid to say a word upon this subject; not for fear of the imputation of being superstitious, but lest I should encourage that disposition in others; and yet it forms a contribution to psychology. So to confess.

"It is acknowledged that the judgment which we form of strangers, on first meeting them, is frequently more correct than that which we adopt upon a longer acquaintance with them. The first impression which, through an instinct of the soul, attracts one towards, or repels one from, another, becomes, after a time, more dim, and is weakened, either through his appearing other than at first, or through our becoming accustomed to him. People speak, too, in reference to such cases of involuntary sympathies and aversions, and attach a special certainty to such manifestations in children, in whom knowledge of mankind by experience is wanting. Others, again, are incredulous, and attribute all to physiognomical skill. But of myself.

"It has happened to me occasionally, at the first meeting with a total stranger, when I have been listening in silence to his conversation, that his past life, up to the present moment, with many minute circumstances belonging to one or other particular scene in it, has come across me like a dream, but distinctly, entirely, involuntarily, and unsought, occupying in duration a few minutes. During this period I am usually so plunged into the representation of the stranger's life, that at last I neither continue to see distinctly his face, on which I was idly speculating, nor to hear intelligently his voice, which at first I was using as a commentary to the text of his physiognomy. For a long time I was disposed to consider these fleeting visions as a trick of the fancy; the more so that my dream-vision displayed to me the dress and movements of the actors, the appearance of the room, the furniture, and other accidents of the scene; till, on one occasion, in a gamesome mood, I narrated to my family the secret history of a sempstress who had just before quitted the room. I had never seen the person before. Nevertheless the hearers were astonished, and laughed, and would not be persuaded but that I had a previous acquaintance with the former life of the person, inasmuch as what I had stated was perfectly true. I was not less astonished to find that my dream-vision agreed with reality. I then gave more attention to the subject, and, as often as propriety allowed of it, I related to those whose lives had so passed before me the substance of my dream-vision, to obtain from them its contradiction or confirmation. On every occasion its confirmation followed, not without amazement on the part of those who gave it.

"Least of all could I myself give faith to these conjuring tricks of my mind. Every time that I described to any one my dream-vision respecting him, I confidently expected him to answer it was not so. A secret thrill always came over me when the listener replied, 'It happened as you say;' or when, before he spoke, his astonishment betrayed that I was not wrong. Instead of recording many instances, I will give one which, at the time, made a strong impression upon me.

"On a fair day, I went into the town of Waldshut, accompanied by two young foresters who are still alive. It was evening, and, tired with our walk, we went into an inn called the Vine. We took our supper with a numerous company at the public table; when it happened that they made themselves merry over the peculiarities and simplicity of the Swiss, in connexion with the belief in Mesmerism, Lavater's physiognomical system, and the like. One of my companions, whose national pride was touched by their raillery, begged me to make some reply, particularly in answer to a young man of superior appearance, who sat opposite, and had indulged in unrestrained ridicule. It happened that the events of this very person's life had just previously passed before my mind. I turned to him with the question, whether he would reply to me with truth and candour, if I narrated to him the most secret passages of his history, he being as little known to me as I to him? That would, I suggested, go something beyond Lavater's physiognomical skill. He promised, if I told the truth, to admit it openly. Then I narrated the events with which my dream-vision had furnished me, and the table learnt the history of the young tradesman's life, of his school years, his peccadilloes, and, finally, of a little act of roguery committed by him on the strong box of his employer. I described the uninhabited room with its white walls, where, to the right of the brown door, there had stood upon the table the small black money-chest, &c. A dead silence reigned in the company during this recital, interrupted only when I occasionally asked if I spoke the truth. The man, much struck, admitted the correctness of each circumstance—even, which I could not expect, of the last. Touched with his frankness, I reached my hand to him across the table, and closed my narrative. He asked my name, which I gave him. We sat up late in the night conversing. He may be alive yet.

"Now I can well imagine how a lively imagination could picture, romance-fashion, from the obvious character of a person, how he would conduct himself under given circumstances. But whence came to me the involuntary knowledge of accessory details, which were without any sort of interest, and respected people who for the most part were utterly indifferent to me, with whom I neither had, nor wished to have, the slightest association? Or was it in each case mere coincidence? Or had the listener, to whom I described his history, each time other images in his mind than the accessory ones of my story, but, in surprise at the essential resemblance of my story to the truth, lost sight of the points of difference? Yet I have, in consideration of this possible source of error, several times taken pains to describe the most trivial circumstances that my dream-vision has shown me.

"Not another word about this strange seer-gift, which I can aver was of no use to me in a single instance, which manifested itself occasionally only, and quite independently of any volition, and often in relation to persons in whose history I took not the slightest interest. Nor am I the only one in possession of this faculty. In a journey with two of my sons, I fell in with an old Tyrolese who travelled about, selling lemons and oranges, at the inn at Unterhauerstein in one of the Jura passes. He fixed his eyes for some time upon me, joined in our conversation, observed that though I did not know him he knew me, and began to describe my acts and deeds, to the no little amusement of the peasants, and astonishment of my children, whom it interested to learn that another possessed the same gift as their father. How the old lemon-merchant acquired his knowledge he was not able to explain to himself nor to me. But he seemed to attach great importance to his hidden wisdom."*

In the newness of such knowledge, it is worth while to note separately each of the particulars which attended the manifestation of this strange mental faculty, with his account of which Zschokke has enriched psychology.

1. Then, after the power of looking up the entire recollections of another, through some other channel than

* Zschokke told a friend of mine at Frankfort, in 1847, shortly before his death, which took place at an advanced age, that in the latter years of his life his seer-gift had never manifested itself.

ordinary inquiry and observation—and as it seemed *directly*—we may note,—

2. The rapidity, minuteness, and precision, which characterized the act of inspection.

3. The feeling attending it of becoming absent or lost to what was going on around.

4. Its involuntariness and unexpectedness.

5. Its being practicable on some only; and

6. Those entire strangers, and at their first interview with the seer.

At present I shall avail myself of the first broad fact alone, remarking, however, of the conditions observed in it, that they clearly indicate the existence of a law on which the phenomenon depended. And I shall assume it to be proved by the above crucial instance, that the mind, or soul, of one human being can be brought, in the natural course of things, and under physiological laws hereafter to be determined, into immediate relation with the mind of another living person.

If this principle be admitted, it is adequate to explain all the puzzling phenomena of real ghosts and of true dreams. For example, the ghostly and intersomnial communications, with which we have as yet dealt, have been announcements of the deaths of absent parties. Suppose our new principle brought into play; the soul of the dying person is to be supposed to have come into direct communication with the mind of his friend, with the effect of suggesting his present condition. If the seer be dreaming, the suggestion shapes a corresponding dream; if he be awake, it originates a sensorial illusion. To speak figuratively, *merely figuratively*, in reference to the circulation of this partial mental obituary, I will suppose that the death of a human being throws a sort of gleam through the spiritual world, which may now and then touch with light some fittingly disposed object; or even two simultaneously, if chance have placed them in the right relation;—as the twin-spires of a cathedral may be momentarily illuminated by some far-off flash, which does not break the gloom upon the roofs below.

The same principle is applicable to the explanation of the vampyr visit. The soul of the buried man is to be supposed to be brought into communication with his friend's mind. Thence follows, as a sensorial illusion, the apparition of the buried man. Perhaps the visit may have been an instinctive effort to draw the attention of his friend to his living grave. I beg to suggest that it would not be an act of superstition *now*, but of ordinary humane precaution, if one dreamed pertinaciously of a recently buried acquaintance, or saw his ghost, to take immediate steps to have the state of the body ascertained.

It is not my intention, in the present letter, to push the application of this principle further. With slight modifications it might be brought to explain several other wonderful stories, which we usually neglect just from not seeing how to explain them. One class of these instances is what was termed second-sight. The belief in it formerly prevailed in Scotland, and in the whole of the north of Europe. But the faculty, if it ever existed, seems to be disappearing now. However, it is difficult, one has heard so many examples of the correctness of its warnings and anticipations, not to believe that it once really manifested itself.

A much respected Scottish lady, not unknown in literature, told me very recently how a friend of her mother, whom she perfectly remembered, had been compelled to believe in second-sight through its occurrence in one of her servants. She had a cook, who was a continual annoyance to her through her possession of this gift. On one occasion, when the lady expected some friends, she learned, a short time before they were to arrive, that the culinary preparations she had ordered to honour them had not been made. Upon her remonstrating with the offending cook, the latter simply but doggedly assured her that come they would not; that she knew it to a certainty; and, true enough, they did not come. Some accident had occurred to prevent their visit. The same person frequently knew beforehand what her mistress's plans were, and was as inconvenient in her kitchen as a calculating prodigy in a counting-house. Things went perfectly right, but the manner was irregular and provoking; so her mistress turned her away. Supposing this story true, the phenomena look just a modification of Zschokke's seer-gift.

A number of incidents there are turning up, for the most part on trivial occasions, which we put aside for fear of being thought superstitious, because as yet a natural solution is not at hand for them. Sympathy in general, the spread of panic fears, the simultaneous occurrence of the same thoughts to two persons, the intuitive knowledge of mankind possessed by some, the magnetic fascination of others, may eventually be found to have to do with a special and unsuspected cause. Among anecdotes of no great conclusiveness that I have heard narrated of this sort, I will cite two of Lord Nelson, told by the late Sir Thomas Hardy to the late Admiral the Hon. G. Dundas, from whom I heard them. The first was mentioned to exemplify Nelson's quick insight into character. Captain Hardy was present as Nelson gave directions to the commander of a frigate to make sail with all speed—to proceed to certain points, where he was likely to fall in with the French fleet—having seen the French, to go to a certain harbour, and there await Lord Nelson's coming. After the commander had left the cabin, Nelson said to Hardy, "He will go to the West Indies, he will see the French; he will go to the harbour I have directed him to; but he will not wait for me—he will sail for England." The commander did so. Shortly before the battle of Trafalgar an English frigate was in advance, looking out for the enemy; her place in the offing was hardly discernible. Of a sudden Nelson said to Hardy, who was at his side, "The Celeste," (or whatever the frigate's name was,) "the Celeste sees the French." Hardy had nothing to say on the matter. "She sees the French; she'll fire a gun." Within a little time, the boom of the signal-gun was heard.*

I am not sure that my new principle will be a general favourite. It will be said that the cases, in which I suppose it manifested, are of too trivial a nature to justify so novel a hypothesis. My answer is, the cases are few and trivial only because the subject has not been attended to. For how many centuries were the laws of electricity preindicated by the single fact that a piece of amber, when rubbed, would attract light bodies! Again, the school of physiological materialists will of course be opposed to it. They hold that the mind is but a function

* The following anecdote has no conceivable right to be introduced on the present occasion; but I had it on the same authority, and it is a pity it should be lost. As our fleet was bearing down upon the enemies' line at Trafalgar, Nelson paced the quarter-deck of the Victory with Sir Thomas Hardy. After a short silence, touching his left thigh with his remaining hand, Nelson said, "I'd give that, Hardy, to come out of this."

or product of the brain, and cannot therefore consistently admit its separate action. But their fundamental tenet is unsound, even upon considering the analogies of matter alone.

What is meant by a product?—in what does production consist? Let us look for instances: a metal is produced from an ore; alcohol is produced from saccharine matter; the bones and sinews of an animal are produced from its food. Production, in the common signification of the word, means the conversion of one substance into another, weight for weight, agreeably with, or under, mechanical, chemical, and vital laws. I speak, of course, of material production. But the case of thought is parallel. The products of the poet's brain are but recombinations of former ideas. Production, with him, is but a rearrangement of the elements of thought. His food may turn into or produce new brain; but it is the mental impressions he has stored which turn into new imagery. To say that the brain turns into thought, is to assert that consciousness and the brain are one and the same thing, which would be an idle abuse of language.

It is indeed true that, with the manifestation of each thought or feeling, a corresponding decomposition of the brain takes place. But it is equally true that, in a voltaic battery in action, each movement of electric force developed there is attended with a waste of the metal-plates which help to form it. But that waste is not converted into electric fluid. The exact quantity of pure zinc which disappears may be detected in the form of sulphate of zinc. The electricity was *not produced, it was only set in motion*, by the chemical decomposition. Here is the true material analogy of the relation of the brain to the mind. Mind, like electricity, is an imponderable force pervading the universe: and there happen to be known to us certain material arrangements, through which each may be influenced. We cannot, indeed, pursue the analogy beyond this step. Consciousness and electricity have nothing further in common. Their further relations to the dissimilar material arrangements, through which they may be excited or disturbed, are subjects of totally distinct studies, and resolvable into laws which have no affinity, and admit of no comparison.

It is singular how early in the history of mankind the belief in the separate existence of the soul developed itself as an instinct of our nature.

Timarchus, who was curious on the subject of the demon of Socrates, went to the cave of Trophonius to consult the oracle about it. There, having for a short time inhaled the mephitic vapour, he felt as if he had received a sudden blow on the head, and sank down insensible. Then his head appeared to him to open, and to give issue to his soul into the other world; and an imaginary being seemed to inform him that "the part of the soul engaged in the body, entrammelled in its organization, is the soul as ordinarily understood; but that there is another part or province of the soul which is the daimon. This has a certain control over the bodily soul, and among other offices constitutes conscience."—"In three months," the vision added, "you will know more of this." At the end of three months Timarchus died.

LETTER V.

TRANCE.—Distinction of esoneural and exoneural mental phenomena—Abnormal relation of the mind and nervous system possible —Insanity—Sleep—Essential nature of Trance—Its alliance with spasmodic seizures—General characters of Trance—Enumeration of its kinds.

THE time has now arrived for expounding the phenomena of Trance; an acquaintance with which is necessary to enable you to understand the source and nature of the delusions with which I have yet to deal.

You have already had glimpses of this condition. Arnod Paole was in a trance in the cemetery of Meduegna—Timarchus was in a trance in the cave of Trophonius.

Let me begin by developing certain preliminary conceptions relating to the subject.

I. Common observation, the spontaneous course of our reflections, our instinctive interpretation of nature, reveal to us matter, motion, and intelligence, as the co-existing phenomena of the universe. In the farthest distances of space cognisable to our senses, we discern matter and motion, and their subordination to intelligence. Upon the earth's surface we discern, in the finely designed mechanism of each plant, the agency of life; and we recognise in the microcosm of each animal a living organization, fitted to be the recipient of individual consciousness, or of personal being.

II. The intelligence which is communicated to living beings becomes, to a great extent, dependent upon the organization with which it is combined. Thus every mental faculty is found to have its definite seat and habitat in the bodily frame. The principal successes of modern physiologists have been achieved in determining with what precise parts of the nervous system each affection of consciousness is functionally associated. Different classes of nerves are found to be appropriated to sensation and volition; different parts of the spinal cord are proved to minister to different offices; and of the subdivisions of the brain, each is thought to correspond with a separate faculty, or sentiment, or appetite. So far the mental forces, or operations of a living human being, may be conceived to be essentially esoneural, (εσω νευρον.) Each appears to have its proper and special workshop or laboratory in the nervous system.

III. But there are not wanting facts which make it reasonable to think that our mental forces or operations transcend occasionally and partially the limits of our corporeal frame. The phenomena adverted to in the preceding letter, in connexion with the narrative of Zschokke's seer-gift, hardly seem to admit of explanation on any other supposition. Nor is it a very improbable conjecture, that phenomena of the same class form, as it were, the complements of many ordinary esoneural operations. Possibly in common perception the mind directly reaches the object perceived, being excited thereto by the antecedent material impressions on our organs, and the sensations which follow. To denote mental phenomena of the kind I am supposing, I propose the term exoneural, (εξω νευρον.) I venture even, following out this idea, to conjecture further, that the Od force may somehow furnish the dynamic bridge along which our exoneural apprehension travels.

IV. The affections of consciousness would thus be in

part esoneural, in part exoneural, during the healthy and normal state of our being; the esoneural part being executed in immediate connexion with its appropriate organ, and every manifestation of it being attended with a physical change in the latter.

V. But it is conceivable, on the assumption of mind being a separate principle from matter, that the human soul may be capable of retaining its union with the body in a new, unusual, and abnormal relation. The hypothesis is startling enough. I adopt it only from seeing no other way of accounting for certain facts which, with the evidence of their reality, will presently be brought forward. I venture to suppose that the mind of a living man may energize abnormally in two ways: first, that a much larger share of its operations may be conducted exoneurally—that is, out of the body—than usual; secondly, that the esoneural mental functions may be conducted within the body in unaccustomed organs, deserting those naturally appropriated to them. Two or three instances have been already given, which favour, at all events, the supposition of the possibility of such an abnormal relation between the mind and the body being realized. But in most of the instances hitherto adverted to, the normal relation may be supposed to have remained.

VI. Thus all the ordinary phenomena of sensorial illusions at once are esoneural, and suppose the persistence of the normal relation of mind and body. The material organ to which the physical agencies preceding sensation are propagated being irritated, is to be supposed to excite in the mind sensuous recollections or fancies that are so vivid as to appear realities.

VII. In mental delusions, again, there is no reason for surmising the intervention of the abnormal relation. But what are mental delusions? They are a part of insanity. And what is insanity? I will summarily state its features; for some of the instances which remain for explanation are referrible to it, and because I delight to crush a volume into a paragraph.

The phenomena of insanity may be arranged under five heads: The first, the insane temperament; the next three the fundamental forms of mental derangement; the fifth, the paroxysmal state. The features of the insane temperament are various; some of them are incompatible with the simultaneous presence of others. When a group of them is present, as a change in natural character, without insanity, insanity is threatened: no form of insanity manifests itself without the presence of some of them. The features of the insane temperament are these: The patient withdraws his sympathies from those around him, is shy, reserved, cunning, suspicious, with a troubled air, as if he felt something to be wrong, and wonders if you see it; he is capricious, and has flaws of temper; being talkative, he is flighty and extravagant; he is hurried in his thoughts, and mode of speaking, and gestures; he has fits of absence, in which he talks aloud to himself; he is restless, and anxious for change of place. Of the elementary forms of insanity, one consists in the entertainment of mental delusions: the patient imagines himself the Deity, or a prophet, or a monarch, or that he has become enormously wealthy; or that he is possessed by the devil, or is persecuted by invisible beings, or is dead, or very poor, or that he is the victim of public or private injustice. The second form is moral perversion: the patient is depressed in spirits without a cause, perhaps to the extent of meditating suicide; or he feels an unaccountable desire to take the lives of others; or he is impelled to steal, or to do gratuitous mischief; or he is a sot; or he has fits of ungovernable and dangerous rage. The third form exhibits itself in loss of connexion of ideas, failure of memory, loss of common intelligence, disregard of the common decencies of life. Each of these three elementary forms is sometimes met with alone; generally two are combined. Sensorial illusions are common in insanity; auditory, unaccompanied by visual illusions, are almost peculiar to it, and to the cognate affection of delirium from fever or inflammation of the brain. To the head of the paroxysmal state belongs the history of exacerbations of insanity, of their sudden outbursts in persons of the insane temperament, of their preferential connexion with this or that antecedent condition of the patient, of their occasional periodicity.

VII. In congenital idiotcy and imbecility, the relation of the mind and brain is normal. Often the defective organization is apparent through which the intelligence is repressed. In many countries a popular belief prevails that the imbecile have occasional glimpses of higher knowledge. There is no reason evident why their minds should not be susceptible of the abnormal relation.

VIII. In sleep, the mind and brain are in the normal relation. But what is sleep, psychically considered?

It is best to begin by looking into the mental constituents of waking. There is then passing before us an endless current of images and reflections, furnished from our recollections, and suggested by our hopes and our fears, by pursuits that interest us, or by their own inter-associations. This current of thought is continually being changed or modified, through impressions made upon our senses. It is further liable to be still more importantly and systematically modified by the exercise of the faculty of Attention. The attention operates in a twofold manner. It enables us to detain at pleasure any subject of thought before the mind; and, when not on such urgent duty, it vigilantly inspects every idea which presents itself, and reports if it be palpably unsound or of questionable tendency. To speak with more precision, it is a power we have of controlling our thoughts, which we drill to warn us whenever the suggested ideas conflict with our experience or our principles.

Then of sleep. We catch glimpses of its nature at the moments of falling asleep and of waking. When it is the usual time for sleep, if our attention happen to be livelily excited, it is in vain we court sleep. When we are striving to contend against the sense of overwhelming fatigue, what we feel is, that we can no longer command our attention. Then we are lost, or are asleep. Then the head and body drop forwards; we have ceased to attend to the maintenance of our equilibrium. Any iteration of gentle impressions, enough to divert attention from other objects, without arousing it, promotes sleep.

Thus we recognise as the psychical basis of sleep the suspension of the attention.

Are any other mental faculties suspended in sleep? Sensation and the influence of the will over the muscular system are not; for our dreams are liable to be shaped by what we hear. The sleeper, without waking, will turn his head away from a bright light, will withdraw his arm if you pinch it, will utter loud words which he dreams he is employing. The seeming insensibility in sleep, the apparent suspension of the influence of the will, are simply consequences of the suspension of attention.

I have, on another occasion, shown that the organs in

which sensations are realized, and volition energizes, are the segments of the cranio-spinal cord in which the sentient and voluntary nerves are rooted. I think I see now that the seat of the attention is the "medulla oblongata." For—alas for the imperfect conceptions into which the imperfection of language as an instrument of thought forces us!—what is the faculty of attention, which we have been considering almost as a separate element of mind, but the individual "ich" energizing, now keenly noticing impressions and thoughts, now allowing them to pass, while it looks on with lazy indifference; now, at length, worn out and exhausted, and incapable of further work? But this inspecting and contrasting operation, where should it more naturally find its bureau than at a point situated between the organs of the understanding and those of the will?—that is to say, somewhere at the junction of the spinal marrow and the brain. Well, Magendie ascertained that just at that region there is a small portion of nervous matter, pressure upon which causes immediately heavy sleep or stupor, while its destruction—*for instance, the laceration of the little organ with the point of a needle*—instantaneously and irrevocably extinguishes life.* This precious link in our system is, reasonably enough, stowed away in the securest part of our frame—that is to say, within the head, upon the strong central bone of the base of the skull. How came the fancy of Shakspeare by the happy figure which seems to adumbrate Magendie's discovery of to-day, in poetry written three hundred years ago?

* The reader who wishes to pursue this subject farther, will find it expounded, in connexion with a large body of collateral facts, in my work entitled *The Nervous System and its Functions.* Parker, West Strand: 1842.

"Within the hollow crown,
That rounds the mortal temples of a king,
Keeps Death his court; and there the antic sits
Mocking his state, and grinning at his pomp;
Allowing him a breath, a little hour,
To monarchize, be feared, and kill with looks;
Infusing him with self and vain conceits,
As if the flesh that walls about our life
Were brass impregnable. Till, humoured thus,
He comes at last, and, with a little pin,
Bores through his castle wall—and farewell king!"

To return to our argument, Are the sentiments and higher faculties of the mind suspended during sleep? Certainly not, if dreaming be a part of natural sleep, as I hold it to be. For there are some who dream always; others, who say they seldom dream; others, who disavow dreaming at all. But the simplest view of these three cases is to suppose that in sleep all persons always dream, but that all do not remember their dreams. This imputed forgetfulness is not surprising, considering the importance of the attention to memory, and that in sleep the attention is suspended. Ordinary dreams present one remarkable feature; nothing in them appears wonderful. We meet and converse with friends long dead; the improbability of the event never crosses our minds. One sees a horse galloping by, and calls after it as one's friend—Mr. so-and-so. We fly with agreeable facility, and explain to an admiring circle how we manage it. Every absurdity passes unchallenged. The attention is off duty. It is important to remark that there is nothing in common dreams to interfere with the purpose of sleep, which is repose. The cares and interests of our waking life never recur to us; or, if they do, are not recognised as our own. The faculties are not really energizing;

their seeming exercise is sport; they are unharnessed, and are gambolling and rolling in idle relaxation. That is their refreshment.

The attention alone slumbers; or, through some slight organic change, it is unlinked from the other faculties, and they are put out of gear. This is the basis of sleep. The faculties are all in their places; but the attention is off duty; itself asleep, or indolently keeping watch of time alone.

In contrast with this picture of the sleeping and waking states, of the alternation of which our mental life consists, I have now to hold up to view another conception, resembling it, but different, vague, imposing, of gigantic proportions, the monstrous double of the first—like the mocking spectre of the Hartz, which yet is but your own shadow cast by the level sunbeams on the morning mist.

To answer to this conception, there is more than the ideal entity made up of the different forms of trance. For although trance may occur as a single sleep-like fit of moderate duration, yet it more frequently recurs—often periodically, dividing the night or day with common sleep or common waking; or it may be persistent for days and weeks—in which case, if it generally maintain one character, it is yet liable to have wakings of its own.

Then the first division of trance is into trance-sleep and trance-waking. In extreme cases it is easy to tell trance-sleep from common sleep, trance-waking from common waking; but there are varieties with less prominent features, in which it is difficult, at first, to say whether the patient is entranced at all.

There is, upon the whole, more alliance between sleep

and trance, than between waking and trance. Or, in a large class of cases, the patient falls into trance when asleep. It is a cognate phenomenon to this that the common initiatory stage of trance is a trance-sleep.

Trance is of more frequent occurrence among the young than among the middle-aged or old people. It occurs more frequently among young women than among young men. In other words, the liability to trance is in proportion to delicacy of organization, and higher nervous susceptibility.

But what is trance? The question will be best answered by exhibiting its several phases. In the mean time, it may be laid down that the basis of trance is the supervention of the abnormal relation of the mind and nervous system. In almost all its forms it is easy to show that some of the mental functions are no longer located in their pristine organs. The most ordinary change is the departure of common sensation from the organ of touch. Next, sight leaves the organs of vision. To make up for these desertions, if the patient wake in trance, either the same senses re-appear elsewhere, or some unaccountable mode of general perception manifests itself.

A strict alliance exists between trance and the whole family of spasms. Most of them are exclusively developed in connexion with it; all are liable to be combined with it; they are all capable of being excited by the same influences which produce trance; so they often occur vicariously, or alternate with trance. One kind is catalepsy; the body motionless, statue-like, but the tone of spasm maintained low, so that you may arrange the statue in what attitude you will, and it preserves it. A second is catochus, like the preceding, but with a higher power of spasm, so that the joints are rigidly fixed; and if you overcome one for a moment with superior strength, being let go, it flies back to where it was. A third, partial spasm of equal rigidity, arching the body forwards or backwards or laterally, or fixing one limb or more. The fourth, clonic spasm, for instance, the contortions and convulsive struggles of epilepsy. The fifth, an impulse to rapid and varied muscular actions, nearly equalling convulsions in violence, but combined so as to travesty ordinary voluntary motion; this is the dance of St. Veitz, which took its name from an epidemic outbreak in Germany in the thirteenth century, that was supposed to be cured by the interposition of the saint; then persons of all classes were seized in groups in public with a fury of kicking, shuffling, dancing together, till they dropt. Now, the same agency is manifested either in a violent rush, and disposition to climb with inconceivable agility and precision; or alternately to twist the features, roll the neck, and jerk and swing the limbs even to the extent of dislocating them.

The causes of trance are mostly mental. Trance appears to be contagious. Viewed medically, it is seldom directly dangerous. It is a product of over-excitability, which time blunts. The disposition to trance is seldom manifested beyond a few months, or, at most, two or three years. For epilepsy is not a form of trance; it is, however, a mixed mental and spasmodic seizure, much allied to trance. Those who suffer from its attacks are found to be among the most susceptible of induced trance.

But let me again ask, what then is trance?

Trance is a peculiar mental seizure, (totally distinct from insanity, with which again, however, it may be combined,) the patient taken with which appears profoundly absorbed or rapt, and as if lost more or less completely to surrounding objects or impressions, or at all events to the ordinary mode of perceiving them; he is likewise more or less entirely lost to his former recollections. The mental seizures may or may not occur simultaneously or alternately with spasmodic seizures of any and every character.

This definition of trance conveys, I am afraid, no very exact or distinct picture; but it is the definition of a genus, and a genus is necessarily an abstraction. However, it gives the features essential to all the forms of trance. A true general notion of trance can, indeed, only be realized by studying in detail each of the forms it includes. These are separated by the broadest colours. In the one extreme an entranced person appears dead, and no sign of life is recognisable in him; in the opposite, he appears to be much as usual, and perfectly impressible by any thing around him, so that it demands careful observation to establish that he is not simply awake.

Then trance presents no fewer than five specific forms, distinguished each from the other by clear characters, their essential identity being established by each at times passing into either of the others. The terms by which I propose to designate the five primary forms of trance are—Death-trance, Trance-coma, Initiatory Trance, Half-waking-trance, Waking-trance. The five, however, admit, as I have before said, of being arranged in two groups: the first three forms enumerated constituting varieties of trance-sleep; the two latter constituting varieties of waking-trance. The next letter will treat of the first group; the two following will treat of the two varieties of the second.

I have observed that the causes of trance are for the most part mental impressions; but it will be found that certain physical influences may produce the same results. The causes of trance, whether mental or physical, deserve again to be regarded in three lights. Either they have operated blindly and fortuitously, or they have been resorted to and used as agents to produce some vague and imperfectly understood result, or they have been skilfully and intelligently directed to bring out the exact phenomena which have followed. It is with trance supervening in the two former ways that I alone propose at present to deal; that is to say, with trance as it was imperfectly known as an agent in superstition, or as a rare and marvellous form of nervous disease. Of the third case of trance, as it may be artificially induced, I shall afterwards and finally speak.

LETTER VI.

TRANCE-SLEEP—The phenomena of trance divided into those of trance-sleep, and those of trance-waking—Trance-sleep presents three forms; trance-waking two. The three forms of trance-sleep described: viz., death-trance, trance-coma, simple or initiatory trance.

TRANCE, then, it appears, is a peculiar mental seizure liable to supervene in persons of an irritable nervous system, either after mental excitement or in deranged bodily health. The seizure may last for a few hours, or a few days, or for weeks, or years; and is liable to recur at regular or irregular intervals.

Trance again, it has been observed, has phases corresponding with the sleeping and waking of our natural state. And as natural sleep presents three varieties—the profound and heavy sleep of extreme exhaustion, ordinary deep sleep, and the light slumber of the wakeful and the anxious, so trance-sleep is three-fold likewise. But as in trance every thing is magnified, the differences between the three states are greater, and the phenomena of each more bold and striking.

Two conditions are common, however, to every phase of trance-sleep; these are, the occurrence of complete insensibility, and that of vivid and coherent dreams.

The insensibility is so absolute that the most powerful stimulants are insufficient to rouse the patient. An electric shock, a surgical operation, the amputation even of a limb, are seemingly unfelt.

The dreams of trance-sleep have a character of their own. It is to be remarked, that in the dreams of ordinary sleep the ideas are commonly an incoherent jumble; and that, if they happen to refer to passing events, they commonly reverse their features. The attention seems to be slumbering. Thus Sir George Back told me, that in the privations which he encountered in Sir John Franklin's first expedition, when in fact he was starving, he uniformly dreamed of plentiful repasts. But in the dreams of trance-sleep, on the contrary, the impressions of the waking thoughts, the exciting ideas themselves, which have caused the supervention of trance, are realized and carried out in a consecutive train of imaginary action. They are, accordingly, upon the patient's awaking, accurately remembered by him; and that with such force and distinctness, that if he be a fanatic or superstitiously inclined, he very likely falls into the belief that the occurrences he dreamed of actually took place in his presence. A temperate fanatic goes no further, under such circumstances, than to assert that he has had a vision. The term is so good a one, that it appears to me worth retaining, in a philosophical sense, for the present exigency. I propose to restrict the term vision to the dreams of persons in trance-sleep.

Then of the three different forms of trance-sleep,

I. *Death-trance.*—Death-trance is the image of death. The heart does not act; the breathing is suspended; the body is motionless; not the slightest outward sign of sensibility or consciousness can be detected. The temperature of the body falls. The entranced person has the appearance of a corpse from which life has recently departed. The joints are commonly relaxed, and the whole frame pliable; but it is likely that spasmodic rigidity forms an occasional adjunct of this strange condition. So the only means of knowing whether life be still present is to wait the event. The body is to be kept in a warm room, for the double purpose of promoting decomposition if it be dead, and of preserving in it the vital spark if it still linger; and it should be constantly watched. But should every recently dead body be made the subject of similar care? it is natural to ask. There are, of course, many cases where such care is positively unnecessary—such, for instance, as death following great lesions of vital organs; and in the great majority of cases of seeming death, the bare possibility of the persistence of life hardly remains. Still it is better to err on the safe side. And although in England, from the higher tone of moral feeling, and from the respect shown to the remains of the dead, the danger of being interred alive is inconsiderable, still the danger certainly exists to a very considerable degree of being opened alive by order of a zealous coroner. But for the illustration of this danger, and examples of the circumstances under which death-trance has been known to occur, and of its usual features, I refer the reader back to the second Letter of this series. Let me, however, add, that it is not improbable that, by means of persons susceptible of the influence of Od, or of persons in induced waking-trance, the question could be at once decided whether a seeming corpse were really dead.

In England, during the last epidemic visitation of cholera, several cases of death-trance occurred, in which the patient, who was on the point of being buried, fortunately awoke in time to be saved. Death-trance, it is probable, is much more frequently produced by spasmodic and nervous illness than by mental causes: it has followed fever; it has frequently attended parturition. In this respect it differs from other forms of trance-sleep, which mostly, when spontaneous, supervene upon mental impressions.

The only feature of death-trance which it remains for me to exemplify is the occurrence in it of visions. Perhaps the following may be taken as an instance:—

Henry Engelbrecht, as we learn in a pamphlet published by him in 1639, after an ascetic life, during which he had experienced sensorial illusions, fell into the deepest form of trance, which he thus describes: In the year 1623, exhausted by intense mental excitement of a religious kind, and by abstinence from food, after hearing a sermon which strongly affected him, he felt as if he could combat no longer; so he gave in and took to his bed.

There he lay a week, without tasting any thing but the bread and wine of the sacrament. On the eighth day, he thought he fell into the death-struggle. Death seemed to invade him from below upwards. His body became to his feelings rigid; his hands and feet insensible; his tongue and lips incapable of motion; gradually his sight failed him. But he still heard the laments and consultations of those around him. This gradual demise lasted from mid-day till eleven at night, when he heard the watchmen. Then he wholly lost sensibility to outward impressions. But an elaborate vision of immense detail began; the theme of which was, that he was first carried down to hell, and looked into the place of torment; from whence, after a time, quicker than an arrow he was borne to Paradise. In these abodes of suffering and happiness, he saw and heard and smelt things unspeakable. These scenes, though long in apprehension, were short in time; for he came enough to himself, by twelve o'clock, again to hear the watchmen. It took him another twelve hours to come round entirely. His hearing was first restored; then his sight; feeling and power of motion followed; as soon as he could move his limbs, he rose. He felt himself stronger than before the trance.

II. *Trance-coma.*—The appearance of a person in trance-coma is that of one in profound sleep. The breathing is regular, but extremely gentle; the action of the heart the same; the frame lies completely relaxed and flexible, and, when raised, falls in any posture, like the body of one just dead, as its weight determines. The bodily temperature is natural. The condition is distinguishable from common sleep by the total insensibility of the entranced person to all ordinary stimulants:

besides, the pupil of the eye, instead of being contracted to a minute aperture, as it is in common sleep, is usually dilated; at all events it is not contracted, and it is fixed.

Perhaps the commonest cause of trance-coma is hysteria; or by hysteria is meant a highly irritable state of the nervous system, most commonly met with in young unmarried women. There seems to be present, as its proximate cause, an excessive nervous vitality; and that excess, in its simplest manifestation, breaks out in fits of sobbing and crying, alternating often with laughter—a physical excitement of the system which yet fatigues and distresses the patient's mind, who cannot resist the unaccountable impulses. It is at the close of such a paroxysm of hysteria that trance-coma of a few hours' duration not unfrequently supervenes. It is almost a natural repose after the preceding stage of excitement. Hysteria, besides giving origin to a peculiar class of local ailments, is further the fruitful mother of most varieties of trance.

Trance-coma sometimes supervenes on fever, and the patient lies for hours or days on the seeming verge of death. I have known it ensue after mesmeric practice carried to an imprudent excess. Religious mental excitement will bring it on. In the following instance, which I quote from the Rev. George Sandby's sensible and useful work on Mesmerism, the state of trance so supervening was probably trance-coma: "George Fox, the celebrated father of Quakerism, at one period lay in a trance for fourteen days, and people came to stare and wonder at him. He had the appearance of a dead man; but his sleep was full of divine visions of beauty and glory."

Here is another instance, wherein the prevailing state must have been trance-coma. I quote it from the letter of an intelligent friend. It will help the reader to realize the general conception I wish to raise in his mind:—

"I heard," says my correspondent, "through the newspapers, of a case of trance ten miles from this place, and immediately rode to the village to verify it, and gain information about it. With some difficulty I persuaded the mother to allow me to see the entranced girl. Her name is Ann Cromer; she is daughter of a mason at Faringdon Gournay, ten miles from Bristol. She was lying in a state of general but not total suspension of the symptoms of life. Her breathing was perceptible by the heaving of the chest, and at times she had uttered low groans. Her jaws are locked, and she is incapable of the slightest movement, so as to create no other wrinkle in her bed-clothes but such as a dead weight would produce. When I saw her, she had not been moved for a week. Upon one occasion, when asked to show, by the pressure of the hand, if she felt any pain, a slight squeeze was perceptible. A very small portion of fluid is administered as food from time to time, but I neglected to discover how. Her hands are warm, and her mother thinks that she is conscious. Three days before I saw her, she spoke (incoherently) for the first time since her trance commenced. She repeated the Lord's prayer, and asked for an aunt; but she rapidly relapsed, and her locked-jaw returned. Her mother considered this revival a sign of approaching death. The most remarkable feature in the case is the length of time that the girl has remained entranced. She was twelve years old when the fit supervened, and the locked-jaw followed in sixteen weeks afterwards. She is now twenty-five years of age, and will thus, in a month, if alive, have been in this condition for thirteen years. In the mean while she has grown from a child to a woman, though her countenance retains all the appearance of her former age. She is little else than skin and bone, except her cheeks, which are puffy. She is as pale as a corpse, and her eyes are sunk deep in the sockets."

III. *Simple or Initiatory Trance.*—In the lightest form of trance-sleep, the patient, though perfectly insensible to ordinary impressions, is not necessarily recumbent. If he is sitting when taken, he continues sitting; if previously lying, he will sometimes raise himself up when entranced. His joints are neither relaxed nor rigid: if you raise his arm, or bend the elbow, you experience a little resistance; and immediately after, probably, the limb is restored to its former posture. Such is the ordinary degree of muscular tone present; but either cataleptic immobility, or catochus, may accidentally co-exist with initiatory trance. The patient may even remain standing rapt in his trance. I quote the following classic instance from the *Edinburgh Review*:—"There is a wonderful story told of Socrates. Being in military service in the expedition to Potidea, he is reported to have stood for twenty-four hours before the camp, rooted to the same spot and absorbed in deep thought, his arms folded and his eyes fixed upon one object, as if his soul were absent from his body."

It is not my intention to dwell more on this form of trance at present. Various cases, exemplifying its varieties, will be found in the letter on Religious Delusions. It is the commonest product of fanatical excitement. I have called this form initiatory trance, because, in day-somnambulism, it always precedes the half-waking which constitutes that state; and because it is the state into which mesmeric manipulators ordinarily first plunge the patient. Out of this initiatory state I have seen the patient thrown into trance-coma; but the ordinary progress of the experiment is to conduct him in the other direction—that is, towards trance-waking.

LETTER VII.

HALF-WAKING TRANCE OR SOMNAMBULISM.—The same thing with ordinary sleep-walking—Its characteristic feature, the acting of a dream—Cases, and disquisition.

A CURIOUS fate somnambulism has had. While other forms of trance have been either rejected as fictions, or converted to the use of superstition, somnambulism with all its wonders, being at once undeniable and familiar, has been simply taken for granted. While her sisters have been exalted into mystical phenomena, and play parts in history, somnambulism has had no temple raised to her, has had no fear-worship, at the highest has been promoted to figure in an opera. Of a quiet and homely nature, she has moved about the house, not like a visiting demon, but as a maid of all work. To the public the phenomenon has presented no more interest than a soap-bubble, or the fall of an apple.

Somnambulism, as the term is used in England, exactly comprehends all the phenomena of half-waking trance.*

* Many writers employ the term somnambulism to denote indiscriminately several forms of trance, or trance in general. I prefer

The seizure mostly comes on during common sleep. But it may supervene in the daytime; in which case the patient first falls into the lightest form of trance-sleep. After a little, still lost to things around him, he manifests one or more of three impulses: one, to speak, but coherently and to a purpose; a second, to dress, rise, and leave his room with an evident intention of going somewhither; a third, to practise some habitual mechanical employment. In each case he appears to be pursuing the thread of a dream. If he speaks, it is a connected discourse to some end. If he goes out to walk, it is to a spot he contemplates visiting; his general turn is to climb ascents, hills, or the roofs of houses: in the latter case he sometimes examines if the tiles are secure before he steps on them. If he pursues a customary occupation, whether it be cleaning harness or writing music, he finishes his work before he leaves it. He is acting a dream, which is connected and sustained. The attention is keenly awake in this dream, and favours its accomplishment to the utmost. In the mean time the somnambulist appears to be insensible to ordinary impressions, and to take no cognisance of what is going on around him—a light may be held so close to his eyes as to singe his eyebrows without his noticing it—he seems neither to hear nor to taste—the eyelids are generally closed, otherwise the eyes are fixed and vacant. Nevertheless he possesses some means of recognising the objects which are implicated in his dream; he perceives their place, and walks among them with perfect precision. Let me narrate some instances. The first, one of day-somnambulism, exemplifies, at the same time, the transitions to full

restricting it to the peculiar class of cases commonly known as sleep-walking.

waking, which manifest themselves occasionally in the talking form of the trance. The case is from the *Acta Vratisv.* ann. 1722.

A girl, seventeen years of age, was used to fall into a kind of sleep in the afternoon, in which it was supposed, from her expression of countenance and her gestures, that she was engaged in dreams that interested her. (She was then in light trance-sleep, initiatory trance.) After some days she began to speak when in this state. Then if those present addressed remarks to her, she replied very sensibly, but then fell back into her dream discourse, which turned principally upon religious and moral topics, and was directed to warn her friends how a female should live—Christianly, well governed, and so as to incur no reproach. When she sang, which often happened, she heard herself accompanied by an imaginary violin or piano, and would take up and continue the accompaniment upon an instrument herself. She sewed, did knitting, and the like. She imagined, on one occasion, that she wrote a letter upon a napkin, which she folded for the post. Upon waking, she had not the slightest recollection of any thing that had passed. After a few months she recovered.

The following case is from the Hamburgh *Zeitschrift für die gesammte Medicin*, 1848:—

A lad of eleven years of age, at school at Tarbes, was surprised several mornings running at finding himself dressed in bed, though he had undressed himself overnight. Then on the 3d of May he was seen by a neighbour, soon after three in the morning, to go out dressed with his cloak and hat on. She called to him, but he did not answer; and she concluded that he was going to Bagnères with his father. In fact that was the road he took;

and he was afterwards seen by several persons near Bagnères, trudging after a carriage. It rained hard; and they were surprised to see so young a lad travelling at so early an hour; but they thought he probably belonged to the people in the carriage. He reached Bagnères at half past five, having done the distance of five post leagues in two hours and a quarter. He went to the hotel of M. Lafargue, which he had on a former occasion visited with his father, and entered the eating-room. The people of the hotel addressed him. He told them that he had come with his father in a post-chaise, and that they would find his father in the yard busied with the carriage. M. Lafargue went out to look for him. In the mean time the people of the house observed that the boy's remarks were incoherent; so they took off his cloak and cap, when they found that his eyelids were closed, and that he was fast asleep. They led him towards the stove, took off his wet things and his boots without awakening him; but before they had completely undressed him to put him to bed he awoke. The impressions of his dream did not desert him. He complained of having had a bad night; and asked for his father. They told him his father had been obliged to set off again immediately. They put him to bed, and he slept. They sent intelligence to his father, who came to Bagnères. The boy believed, and believes still, that he came to Bagnères with his father in a chaise that was driven very slowly. Being asked what he had seen on the road, he described having passed a number of monks and priests in procession. He said there was one good-looking young man who did not leave him, but was always saying, "Good day, Joseph; Adieu, Joseph." He said that what had most annoyed him was the burning heat of the sun, which was so intense that he had been obliged to wrap himself up in his cloak; that he could not bear its bright light.

The following case of somnambulism, allied with St. Vietz's dance is given by Lord Monboddo:—

The patient, about sixteen years of age, used to be commonly taken in the morning a few hours after rising. The approach of the seizure was announced by a sense of weight in the head and drowsiness, which quickly terminated in sleep, (trance-sleep,) in which her eyes were fast shut. She described a feeling beginning in the feet, creeping like a gradual chill higher and higher, till it reached the heart, when consciousness left her. Being in this state, she sprang from her seat about the room, over tables and chairs, with astonishing agility. Then, if she succeeded in getting out of the house, she ran, at a pace with which her elder brother could hardly keep up, to a particular spot in the neighbourhood, taking the directest but the roughest path. If she could not manage otherwise, she got over the garden wall, with astonishing rapidity and precision of movement. Her eyelids were all the time fast closed. The impulse to visit this spot she was often conscious of during the approach of the paroxysm, and afterwards she sometimes thought that she had dreamed of going thither. Towards the termination of her indisposition, she dreamed that the water of a neighbouring spring would do her good, and she drank much of it. One time they tried to cheat her by giving her water from another spring, but she immediately detected the difference. Near the end, she foretold that she would have three paroxysms more, and then be well; and so it proved.

The next case is from a communication by M. Pigatti, published in the July number of the *Journal Encyclo-*

pedique of the year 1662. The subject was a servant of the name of Negretti, in the household of the Marquis Sale.

In the evening Negretti would seat himself in a chair in the ante-room, when he commonly fell asleep, and would sleep quietly for a quarter of an hour. He then righted himself in his chair so as to sit up. Then he sat some time without motion, looking as if he saw something. Then he rose and walked about the room. On one occasion he drew out his snuff-box, and would have taken a pinch, but there was little in it; whereupon he walked up to an empty chair, and, addressing by name a cavalier, whom he supposed to be sitting in it, asked him for a pinch. One of those who were watching the scene, here held towards him an open box, from which he took snuff. Afterward he fell into the posture of a person who listens; he seemed to think that he heard an order, and thereupon hastened with a wax candle in his hand to a spot where a light usually stood. As soon as he imagined that he had lit the candle, he walked with it in the proper manner, through the *salle*, down the steps, turning and waiting from time to time as if he were lighting some one down. Arrived at the door he placed himself sideways, in order to let the imaginary persons pass; and he bowed as he let them out. He then extinguished the light, returned up stairs, and sat himself down again in his place, to play the same farce once or twice over again the same evening. When in this condition he would lay the table-cloth, place the chairs, which he sometimes brought from a distant room, opening and shutting the doors as he went with exactness; would take decanters from the buffet, fill them with water at the spring, put them down on a waiter, and so on. All the objects that were concerned in these operations he distinguished, when they were before him, with the same precision and certainty as if he had been in the full use of his senses. Otherwise he seemed to observe nothing; so, on one occasion in passing a table, he threw down a waiter with two decanters upon it, which fell and broke without attracting his attention. The dominant idea had entire possession of him. He would prepare a salad with correctness, and sit down and eat it. If they changed it, the trick escaped his notice. In this manner he would go on eating cabbage, or even pieces of cake, without observing the difference. The taste he enjoyed was imaginary, the sense was shut. On another occasion, when he asked for wine they gave him water, which he drank for wine, and remarked that his stomach felt the better for it. On a fellow-servant touching his legs with a stick, the idea arose in his mind that it was a dog, and he scolded to drive it away; but the servant continuing his game, Negretti took a whip to beat the dog. The servant drew back, when Negretti began whistling and coaxing to get the dog near him; so they threw a muff against his legs, which he belaboured soundly.

M. Pigatti watched these proceedings with great attention, and convinced himself by many experiments that Negretti did not use his ordinary senses. He did not hear the loudest sound when it lay out of the circle of his dream-ideas. If a light was held close to his eyes, near enough to singe his eyebrows, he did not appear to be aware of it. He seemed to feel nothing when they inserted a feather into his nostrils.

Perhaps the most interesting case of somnambulism on record is that of a young ecclesiastic, the narrative of which, from the immediate communication of the Archbishop of Bordeaux, is given under the head of Somnambulism, in the *French Encyclopedia.*

This young ecclesiastic, when the archbishop was at the same seminary, used to rise every night, and write out either sermons or pieces of music. To study his condition, the archbishop betook himself several nights consecutively to the chamber of the young man, where he made the following observations:—

The young man used to rise, take paper, and begin to write. Before writing music, he would take a stick and rule the lines with it. He wrote the notes, together with the words corresponding to them, with perfect correctness; or when he had written the words too wide, he altered them. The notes that were to be black he filled in after he had written the whole. After completing a sermon, he would read it aloud from beginning to end. If any passage displeased him, he erased it, and wrote the amended passage correctly over the other. On one occasion he had substituted the word "adorable" for "divin;" but he did not omit to alter the preceding "ce" into "cet," by adding the letter "t" with exact precision to the word first written. To ascertain whether he used his eyes, the archbishop interposed a sheet of pasteboard between the writing and his face. The somnambulist took not the least notice, but went on writing as before. The limitation of his perceptions to what he was thinking about was very curious. A bit of aniseed cake, that he had sought for, he ate approvingly; but when, on another occasion, a piece of the same cake was put into his mouth, he spat it out without observation. The following instance of the dependence of his perceptions upon his preconceived ideas is truly wonderful. It is to be observed that he always knew when his pen had ink in it. Likewise, if they adroitly changed his papers when he was writing, he knew it, if the sheet substituted was of a different size from the former, and he appeared embarrassed in that case. But if the fresh sheet of paper, which was substituted for that written on, was exactly of the same size with it, he appeared not to be aware of the change. And he would continue to read off his composition from the blank sheet of paper, as fluently as when the manuscript lay before him; nay more, he would continue his corrections, and introduce an amended passage, writing it upon exactly the place in the blank sheet corresponding with that which it would have occupied on the written page.—Such are the feats of somnambulists.

At first sight, the phenomena thus exemplified appear strange and unintelligible enough. But upon a careful consideration of them, much of the marvellous disappears. The most curious features seem, in the end, to be really the least deserving of wonder. The simplest of the phenomena are alone the inexplicable ones.

I have, however, advanced this group of cases as instances of trance, in which, therefore, I assume that an abnormal relation exists between the mind and body, in which the organs of sensation are partially or entirely deserted by their functions, and in which new perceptive powers manifest themselves. Then an opponent might argue;—

"I know nothing about your trance. What I see is first a person asleep, then the same person half or partially awake, occupied with a dream or vivid conception of an action; which, being partially awake, and therefore having partially resumed his power of attention, he is capable of realizing. He appears to be insensible; but this may be deceptive; for he is still asleep, and therefore notices not things around him; and his attention is partly still suspended as in sleep, partly more useless still for general purposes through intent preoccupation.

"He goes about the house in his rapt state, and finds his way perfectly; but the house is familiar to him; every thing in it is distinctly before his conception; he has, too, the advantage of perfect confidence; and besides, being partially awake, he partially, vaguely perhaps, uses customary sensations in reference to the objects which his dream contemplates his meeting.

"The ecclesiastic, indeed, seems at first to see through a sheet of pasteboard. But the concluding interesting fact in his case shows that he really used his perception only to identify the size and place of the sheet of paper. His writing upon it was the mechanical transcript of an act of mental penmanship. The corrections fell into the right places upon the paper, owing to the fidelity with which he retained the mental picture. The clearness and vividness of the picture, again, is not so very surprising, when it is considered that the attention was wholly and exclusively concentrated on that one operation."

The observations of my imaginary opponent might sufficiently account for the more striking phenomena in the preceding cases, and are doubtless near the truth as regards the principal parts of the young ecclesiastic's performance. Still there remains the commoner instance of the lad going about with precision with his eyes shut. I see no mode of accounting for that on common principles.

And besides, it may be presumed that, if more decisive experiments as to their sensibility had been made upon all these subjects, they would have been found really without sight and feeling. For, in general character, persons in somnambulism exactly resemble other entranced persons, who certainly feel nothing; for they have borne the most painful surgical operations without the smallest indication of suffering. So I have little doubt that the insensibility, which the observers imputed to the somnambulists, really existed, although they may have failed to establish the fact by positive evidence.

The question as to the development of a new power of perception, such as I conjecture the lad used in his walk from Tarbes to Bagnères, will be found to be resolved, or, at any rate, to be attended with no theoretical difficulties, when the performances of full-waking in trance, which I propose to describe in the next letter, shall have been laid before the reader.

LETTER VIII.

TRANCE-WAKING.—Instances of its spontaneous occurrence in the form of catalepsy—Analysis of catalepsy—Its three elements: double consciousness, or pure waking-trance; the spasmodic seizure; the new mental powers displayed—Cases exemplifying catalepsy—Other cases unattended with spasm, but of spontaneous occurrence, in which new mental powers were manifested—Oracles of antiquity—Animal instinct—Intuition.

UNDER this head are contained the most marvellous phenomena which ever came as a group of facts in natural philosophy before the world; and they are reaching that stage towards general reception when their effect is most vivid and striking. Five-and-twenty years ago no one in England dreamed of believing them, although the same positive evidence of their genuineness then existed as now. Five-and-twenty years hence the same facts will be matters of familiar knowledge. It is just at the present moment (or am I anticipating the march of opinion by half a century?) that their difference, and distinctness, and abhorrence even, from our previous conceptions are most intensely felt; and that the powers which they promise eventually to place within human control excite our irrepressible wonder.

I shall narrate the facts which loom so large in the dawning light, very simply and briefly, as they are manifested in catalepsy.

An uninformed person being in the room with a cataleptic patient, would at first suppose her, putting aside the spasmodic affection of the body, to be simply awake in the ordinary way. By-and-by her new powers might or might not catch his observation. But a third point would certainly escape his notice. I refer to her mental state of waking trance, which gives, as it were, the local colouring to the whole performance.

To elucidate this element, I may avail myself of a sketch ready prepared by nature, tinted with the local colour alone—the case of simple trance-waking, unattended by fits or by any marvellous powers, as far as it has been yet observed, which is known to physicians under the name of double consciousness.

A single fit of the disorder presents the following features:—The young person (for the patient is most frequently a girl) seems to lose herself for a moment or longer, then she recovers, and seems to be herself again. The intervening short period, longer at first, and by use rendered briefer and briefer, is a period of common initiatory trance. When, having lost, the patient thus finds herself again, there is nothing in her behaviour which would lead a stranger to suppose her other than naturally awake. But her friends observe that she now does every thing with more spirit and better than before—sings better, plays better, has more readiness, moves even more gracefully, than in her usual state. She manifests an innocent boldness and disregard of little conventionalisms, which impart a peculiar charm to her behaviour. Her mode of speaking is perhaps something altered; a supernumerary consonant making its undue appearance, but upon a regular law, in certain syllables. But the most striking thing is, that she has totally forgotten all that has passed during the morning. Inquire what her last recollections are, they leave off with the termination of her last fit of this kind; the intervening period is for the present lost to her. She was in her natural state of waking when I introduced her to your notice; she lost herself for a few seconds, found herself again; but found herself not in her natural train of recollections, but in those of the last fit.

These fits occur sometimes at irregular intervals, sometimes periodically and daily. In her ordinary waking state, she has her chain of waking recollections. In her trance-waking state, she has her chain of trance-waking recollections. The two are kept strictly apart. Hence the ill-chosen term, double-consciousness. So at the occurrence of her first fit, her mental existence may be said to have bifurcated into two separate routes, in either of which her being is alternately passed. It is curious to study, at the commencement of such a case, with how much knowledge derived from her past life the patient embarks on her trance-existence. The number of previously realized ideas retained by different patients at the first fit is very various. It has happened that the memory of facts and persons has been so defective that the patient has had to learn even to know and to love her parents. To most of her acquaintances she is observed to give new names, which she uses to them in the trance-state alone. But her habits remain; her usual propriety of conduct: the mind is singularly pure in trance. And she very quickly picks up former ideas, and restores former intimacies, but on a supposed new footing. To complete this curious history, if the fits of trance recur frequently, and through some accidental circumstance are more and more prolonged in duration, so that most of her waking existence is passed in trance, it will follow that the trance-development of her intellect and character may get ahead of their development in her natural waking. Being told this, she may become anxious to continue always in her entranced state, and to drop the other: and I knew a case in which circumstances favoured this final arrangement, and the patient at last retained her trance-recollections alone, from long continuance in that state having made it, as it were, her natural one. Her only fear was—for she had gradually learned her own mental history, as she expressed it to me—that some day she should of a sudden find herself a child again, thrown back to the point at which she ceased her first order of recollections. This is, indeed, a very extreme and monstrous case. Ordinarily, the recurrence of fits of simple trance-waking does not extend over a longer period than three or four months or half a year, after which they never reappear; and her trance acquirements and feelings are lost to the patient's recollection for good. I will cite a case, as it was communicated to me by Dr. G. Barlow, exemplifying some of the points of the preceding statement.

"This young lady has two states of existence. During the time that the fit is on her, which varies from a few hours to three days, she is occasionally merry and in spirits; occasionally she appears in pain, and rolls about in uneasiness; but in general she seems so much herself, that a stranger entering the room would not remark any thing extraordinary: she amuses herself with reading or working, sometimes plays on the piano—and better than at other times—knows every body, and converses rationally, and makes very accurate observations on what she has seen and read. The fit leaves her suddenly, and she then forgets every thing that has passed during it, and imagines that she has been asleep, and sometimes that she has dreamed of any circumstance that has made a vivid impression upon her. During one of these fits she was reading Miss Edgeworth's Tales, and had in the morning been reading a part of one of them to her mother, when she went for a few minutes to the window, and suddenly exclaimed, "Mamma, I am quite well, my headach is gone." Returning to the table, she took up the open volume, which she had been reading five minutes before, and said, "What book is this?" She turned over the leaves, looked at the frontispiece, and replaced it on the table. Seven or eight hours afterwards, when the fit returned, she asked for the book, went on at the very paragraph where she had left off, and remembered every circumstance of the narrative. And so it always is; she reads one set of books during one state, and another during the other. She seems to be conscious of her state; for she said one day, "Mamma, this is a novel, but I may safely read it; it will not hurt my morals, for, when I am well, I shall not remember a word of it."

To form a just idea of a case of catalepsy, the reader has to imagine such a case as I have just instanced, with the physical feature added, that the patient, when entranced, is motionless and fixed as a statue; the spasmodic state, however, not confining itself closely to one type, but running into catochus, or into partial rigid spasm, or into convulsive seizures, (see Letter V.) capriciously.

The psychical phenomena exhibited by the patient when thus entranced, are the following:—

1. The organs of sensation are deserted by their natural sensibility. The patient neither feels with the skin, nor sees with the eyes, nor hears with the ears, nor tastes with the mouth.

2. All these senses, however, are not lost. Sight and hearing, if not smell and taste, reappear in some other part—at the pit of the stomach, for instance, or the tips of the fingers.

3. The patient manifests new perceptive powers. She discerns objects all around her, and through any obstructions, partitions, walls or houses, and at an indefinite distance. She sees her own inside, as it were, illuminated, and can tell what is wrong in the health of others. She reads the thoughts of others, whether present or at indefinite distances. The ordinary obstacles of space and matter vanish to her. So likewise that of time; she foresees future events.

Such and more are the capabilities of cataleptic patients, most of whom exhibit them all—but there is some caprice in their manifestation.

I first resigned myself to the belief that such statements as the above might be true, upon being shown by the late Mr. Bulteel letters from an eminent provincial physician in the year 1838, describing phenomena of this description in a patient the latter was attending. In the spring of 1839, Mr. Bulteel told me that he had himself in the interim often seen the patient, who had allowed him to test in any way he pleased the reality of the faculties she possessed when entranced. As usual, in the hours which she passed daily in her natural state, she had no recollection of her extraordinary trance performances. The following are some of the facts, which Mr. Bulteel told me he had himself verified.

When entranced, the patient's expression of countenance was slightly altered, and there was some peculiarity in her mode of speaking. To each of her friends she had given a new name, which she used only when in the state of trance. She could read with her skin. If she pressed the palm of her hand against the whole surface of a printed or written page deliberately, as it were, to take off an impression, she became acquainted verbally with its contents, even to the extent of criticising the type or the handwriting. One day, after a remark made to put her off her guard, a line of a folded note was pressed against the back of her neck; she had read it. She called this sense-feeling—contact was necessary for its manifestation. But she had a general perceptive power besides. She used to tell that persons, whom she knew, were coming to the house, when they were yet at some distance. Persons sitting in the room with her playing chess, to whom her back was turned, if they made intentionally false moves, she would ask them what they possibly could do that for.

The next three cases which I shall describe are from a memoir on catalepsy (1787) by Dr. Petetin, an eminent civil and military physician at Lyons.

M. Petetin attended a young married lady in a sort of fit. She lay seemingly unconscious; when he raised her arm, it remained in the air where he placed it. Being put to bed, she commenced singing. To stop her, the doctor placed her limbs each in a different position. This embarrassed her considerably, but she went on singing. She seemed perfectly insensible. Pinching the skin, shouting in her ear, nothing aroused her attention. Then it happened that, in arranging her, the doctor's foot slipped; and, as he recovered himself, half leaning over her, he said, "How provoking we can't make her leave off singing!" "Ah, doctor," she cried, "don't be angry! I won't sing any more," and she stopped. But shortly she began again; and in vain did the doctor implore her, by the loudest entreaties, addressed to her ear, to keep her promise and desist. It then occurred to him to place himself in the same position as when she heard him before. He raised the bed-clothes, bent his head towards her stomach, and said, in a loud voice, "Do you, then, mean to sing for ever?" "Oh, what pain you have given me!" she exclaimed; "I implore you speak lower." At the same time she passed her hand over the pit of her stomach. "In what way, then, do you hear?" said Dr. Petetin. "Like any one else," was the answer. "But I am speaking to your stomach." "Is it possible!" she said. He then tried again whether she could hear with her ears, speaking even through a tube to aggravate his voice—she heard nothing. On his asking her, at the pit of her stomach, if she had not heard him,—"No," said she, "I am indeed unfortunate."

A cognate phenomenon to the above is *the conversion of the patient's new sense of vision in a direction inwards.* He looks into himself, and sees his own inside as it were illuminated or transfigured: that is to say, his visual power is turned inwards, and he sees his organs possibly by the Od-light they give out.

A few days after the scenes just described, Dr. Petetin's patient had another attack of catalepsy. She still heard at the pit of her stomach, but the manner of hearing was modified. In the mean time her countenance expressed astonishment. Dr. Petetin inquired the cause. "It is not difficult," she answered, "to explain to you why I look astonished. I am singing, doctor, to divert my attention from a sight which appals me. I see my inside, and the strange forms of the organs, surrounded with a network of light. My countenance must express what I feel—astonishment and fear. A physician who should have my complaint for a quarter of an hour would think himself fortunate, as nature would reveal all her secrets to him. If he was devoted to his profession, he would not, as I do, desire to be quickly well." "Do you see your heart?" asked Dr. Petetin. "Yes, there it is; it beats at twice, the two sides in agreement; when the upper part contracts, the lower part swells, and immediately after that contracts. The blood rushes out all luminous, and issues by two great vessels, which are but a little apart."

One morning (to quote from the latter part of this case) the access of the fit took place, according to custom, at eight o'clock. Petetin arrived later than usual; he announced himself by speaking to the fingers of the patient, (by which he was heard.) "You are a very lazy person this morning, doctor," said she. "It is true, madam; but if you knew the reason, you would not reproach me." "Ah," said she, "I perceive you have had a headache for the last four hours: it will not leave you till six in the evening. You are right to take nothing; no human means can prevent it running its course." "Can you tell me on which side is the pain?" said Petetin.

"On the right side; it occupies the temple, the eye, the teeth: I warn you that it will invade the left eye, and that you will suffer considerably between three and four o'clock; at six you will be free from pain." The prediction came out literally true. "If you wish me to believe you, you must tell me what I hold in my hand." "I see through your hand an antique medal."

Petetin inquired of his patient at what hour her own fit would cease: "At eleven." "And the evening accession—when will it come on?" "At seven o'clock." "In that case it will be later than usual." "It is true; the periods of its recurrence are going to change to so and so." During this conversation, the patient's countenance expressed annoyance. She then said to M. Petetin, "My uncle has just entered; he is conversing with my husband behind the screen; his visit will fatigue me; beg him to go away." The uncle, leaving, took with him by mistake her husband's cloak, which she perceived, and sent her sister-in-law to reclaim it.

In the evening there were assembled, in the lady's apartment, a good number of her relations and friends. Petetin had, intentionally, placed a letter within his waistcoat, on his heart. He begged permission, on arriving, to wear his cloak. Scarcely had the lady, the access having come on, fallen into trance, when she said—"And how long, doctor, has it come into fashion to wear letters next the heart?" Petetin pretended to deny the fact: she insisted on her correctness; and, raising her hands, designated the size, and indicated exactly the place of the letter. Petetin drew forth the letter, and held it, closed, to the fingers of the patient. "If I were not a discreet person," she said, "I should tell the contents; but to show you that I know them, they form exactly two lines and a-half of writing;" which, on opening the letter, was shown to be the fact.

A friend of the family, who was present, took out his purse, and put it in Dr. Petetin's bosom, and folded his cloak over his chest. As soon as Petetin approached his patient, she told him that he had the purse, and named its exact contents. She then gave an inventory of the contents of the pockets of all present, adding some pointed remark when the opportunity offered. She said to her sister-in-law that the most interesting thing in *her* possession was a letter;—much to her surprise, for she had received the letter the same evening, and had mentioned it to no one.

The patient, in the mean time, lost strength daily, and could take no food. The means employed failed of giving her relief, and it never occurred to M. Petetin to inquire of her how he should treat her. At length, with some vague idea that she suffered from too great electric tension of the brain, he tried, fantastically enough, the effect of making deep inspirations, standing close in front of the patient. No effect followed from this absurd proceeding. Then he placed one hand on the forehead, the other on the pit of the stomach of the patient, and continued his inspirations. The patient now opened her eyes; her features lost their fixed look; she rallied rapidly from the fit, which lasted but a few minutes instead of the usual period of two hours more. In eight days, under a pursuance of this treatment, she entirely recovered from her fits, and with them ceased her extraordinary powers. But, during these eight days, her powers manifested a still greater extension; she foretold what was going to happen to her; she discussed with astonishing subtlety, questions of mental philosophy and physiology; she caught what those around her meant to say before they expressed their wishes, and either did what they desired, or begged that they would not ask her to do what was beyond her strength.

A young lady, after much alarm during a revolutionary riot, fell into catalepsy. In her fits she appeared to hear with the pit of the stomach; and most of the phenomena described in the preceding case were again manifested. She improved in health, under the care of Dr. Petetin, up to the 29th of May, 1790, the memorable day when the inhabitants of Lyons expelled the wretches who were making sport of their fortunes, their liberties, and their lives. At the report of the first cannon fired, Mdlle. —— fell into violent convulsions, followed by catalepsy and tetanus. When in this state she discerned Petetin distinguishing himself under the fire of a battery; and she blamed him the following day for having so rashly exposed his life. In the progress of the complaint, during the attacks of catalepsy, the occurrences of which she exactly foresaw, she likewise predicted the bloody day of the 29th of September, the surrender of the city on the 7th of October, the entrance of the republican troops on the 8th, and the cruel proscriptions issued by the Committee of Public Safety.

The third case given by Petetin is that of Madame de Saint Paul, who was attacked with catalepsy a few days after her marriage, in consequence of seeing her father fall down in a fit of apoplexy at table. The general features of her lucidity are the same as in the former cases. I shall, therefore, content myself with quoting some observations made by Dr. Prost, author of *La Médecine éclairée par l'Observation et l'Anatomie pathologique*, on the authority of Dr. Foissac, to whom he communicated them. Dr. Prost had studied this case assiduously during nine months. "Her intellectual faculties," observed Dr. Prost, "acquired a great activity, and the richness of her fancy made itself remarked in the picturesque images which she threw into her descriptions. As she was telling her friends of an approaching attack of catalepsy, suddenly she exclaimed,—'I no longer see or hear objects in the same manner; every thing is transparent round me, and my observation extends to incalculable distances.' She designated, without an error, the people who were on the public promenade, whether near the house, or still a quarter of an hour's walk distant. She read the thoughts of every one who came near her; she marked those who were false and vicious; and repelled the approach of stupid people, who bored her with their questions and aggravated her malady. 'Just as much as their pates excite my pity,' said she, 'do the heads of men of information and intelligence, all whose thoughts I look into, fill me with delight.'"

The following facts I cite corroboratively, from one of several cases of hysteria communicated by Dr. Delpit, inspecting physician of the waters at Barèges.—(*Bibliotheque Médicale*, t. lvi. p. 308.)

Mdlle. V——, aged thirteen, after seeing the curé administer extreme unction, fainted away. There followed extreme disgust towards food. During eighteen days she neither ate nor drank; there was no secretion; her breathing remained tranquil and regular; the patient preserved her embonpoint and complexion. During this complete suspension of the functions of digestion, the organs of sensation would be alternately paralyzed. One day the patient became blind; on the next, she could see, but could not hear; another day she lost her speech. The mutations were noticed generally in the night, upon her waking out of sleep. "Nevertheless," says M. Delpit, "her intellect preserved all its vivacity and force, and, during the palsy of the organs of sensation, nature supplied the loss in another way; when, with her eyes, Mdlle. Caroline could not distinguish light, she yet read, and read distinctly, by carrying her fingers over the letters. I have made her thus read, in the daytime and in the profoundest darkness, either printed pages out of the first book that came to hand, or written passages that I had previously prepared." In this, the alternation of different states of recollections is not described as having been observed. But I have little doubt that double consciousness was really present. I believe that feature to be essential to waking trance. I have little doubt, likewise, that double consciousness is attended by more or less trance perception. The co-existence of spasm, necessary to constitute the case one of catalepsy, is accidental.

Sensorial illusions occasionally occur in catalepsy, but not frequently; they are commoner in the inferior grades of trance. The daimon of Socrates was, no doubt, a hallucination of this kind.

The trance-daimon, or sensorial illusion mixing itself with trance, is exemplified in the following case of catalepsy, which occurred in the person of the adopted daughter of the Baron de Strombeck.

Besides the ordinary features, on which I will not again dwell, at one time it was her custom to apply to an imaginary being for directions as to the treatment of her own case. Subsequently, she one day observed—"It is not a phantom; I was in error in thinking it so; it is a voice which speaks within me, and which I think without me. This apparition comes because my sleep is less perfect. In that case, I seem to see a white cloud rise out of the earth, from which a voice issues, the echo of which reverberates within me."

This patient had quintuple consciousness, or four morbid states, each of which kept its own recollections to itself.

A final case I will quote, the authority of which is the Baron de Fortis. It was treated by Dr. Despine of Aix-les-Bains.

The patient had had epilepsy, for the cure of which she went to Aix. There she had all sorts of fits and day-somnambulism, during which she waited at table, with her eyes shut, perfectly. She likewise saw alternately with her fingers, the palm of her hand, and her elbow, and would write with precision with her right hand, superintending the process with her left elbow. These details are peculiarly gratifying to myself, for in the little I have seen, I yet have seen a patient walk about with her eyes shut, and well blinded besides, holding the knuckles of one hand before her as a seeing lantern. However, the special interest of this case is, that the patient was differently affected by different kinds of matter; glass appeared to burn her, porcelain was pleasantly warm, earthenware felt cold.

What comment can I make on the preceding wondrous details? Those to whom they are new must have time to become familiar with them; in order, reversing the process by which the eye gets to see in the dark, to learn to distinguish objects in this flood of excessive light. Those who are already acquainted with them will, I think, agree with me that the principle which I have assumed—the possibility of an abnormal relation of the mind and body allowing the former, either to shift the place of its manifestations in the nervous system, or partially to energize as free spirit—is the only one which at present offers any solution of the new powers displayed in catalepsy. One regrets that more was not made of the opportunities of observation which Petetin enjoyed. But there are means, which I shall by-and-by have occasion to specify, through which, in the practice of medicine, and in the proper treatment of various disorders, like instances may be artificially multiplied and modified so as to meet the exigencies of inductive science. In the mean time, let me append one or two corollaries to the preceding demonstration.

I. It is evident that the performances of catalepsy reduce the oracles of antiquity to natural phenomena. Let us examine the tradition of that of Delphi.

Diodorus relates, that goats feeding near an opening in the ground were observed to jump about in a singular manner, and that a goatherd approaching to examine the spot was taken with a fit and prophesied. Then the priests took possession of the spot and built a temple. Plutarch tells us that that the priestess was an uneducated peasant-girl, of good character and conduct. Placed upon the tripod, and affected by the exhalation, she struggled and became convulsed, and foamed at the mouth; and in that state she delivered the oracular answer. The convulsions were sometimes so violent that the Pythia died. Plutarch adds, that the answers were never in error, and that their established truth filled the temple with offerings from the whole of Greece, and from barbarian nations. Without supposing it to have been infallible, we must, I think, infer that the oracle was too often right to have been wholly a trick. The state of the Pythia was probably trance with convulsions, the same with that in which cataleptic patients have foreseen future events. The priestess was of blameless life, which suits the production of trance, the fine susceptibility of which is spoilt by irregular living. Finally, from what we know of the effects of the few gases and vapours of which the inhalation has been tried, it is any thing but improbable that one or other gaseous compound should directly induce trance in predisposed subjects.

II. The performances of Zschokke are poor by the side of those of a cataleptic. But then he was not entranced. Nevertheless, an approach to that state manifested itself in his losing himself when inspecting his visiter's brains. So again, those who had the gift of second-sight are represented to have been subject to fits of abstraction, in which they stood rapt. The præternatural gifts of Socrates were probably those of a Highland seer; in which character he is reported to have foretold the death of an officer, if he pursued a route he contemplated. The officer would not change his plans, and was met by the enemy, and slain accordingly. In all these cases, the mind seems to have gone out to seek its knowledge. Two of Mr. Williamson's lucid patients, of whom more afterwards, told him that their minds went out at the backs of their heads, in starting on these occasions. They pointed to the lower and back part of the head, opposite to the medulla oblongata. In prophetic, and in true retrospective dreams, one may imagine the phenomena taking the same course; most likely the dreamers have slipt in their sleep into a brief lucid somnambulism. In the cases of ghosts and of dreams, coincident with the period of the death of an absent person, it seems simpler to suppose the visit to have come from the other side. So the Vampyr-ghost was probably a visit made by the free part of the mind of the patient who lay buried in death-trance. The visit was fatal to the party visited, because trance is contagious.

III. The wonderful performances attributed to instinct in animals appear less incomprehensible when viewed in juxtaposition with some of the feats of lucid cataleptics. The term instinct is a very vague one. It is commonly used to denote the intelligence of animals as opposed to human reason. Instinct is, therefore, a compound phenomenon; and I must begin by resolving it into its elements. They are three in number:—

1. Observation and reasoning of the same kind with that of man, but limited in their scope. They are exercised only in immediate self-preservation, and in the direct supply of the creature's bodily wants or simple impulses. A dog will whine to get admission into the house, will open the latch of a gate; one rook will sit sentry for the rest; a plover will fly low, and short distances, as if hurt, to wile away a dog from her nest. But in this vein of intelligence, animals make no further advance. Reflection, with the higher faculties and sentiments which minister to it, and with it constitute reason, is denied them. So they originate no objects of pursuit in the way that man does, and have no source of self-improvement. But, in lack of human reflection, some animals receive the help of—

2. Special conceptions, which are developed in their minds at fitting seasons. Of this nature, to give an instance, is the notion of nest-building in birds. It may be observed of these conceptions that they appear to us arbitrary, though perfectly suited to the being of each species: thus, in the example referred to, we may suppose that the material and shape of the nest might be varied without its object being the less perfectly attained,—at least, as far as we can see. The conception spontaneously

developed in the mind of the bird is then carried out intelligently, through the same quick and just observation, in a little way, which habitually ministers to its appetites, as I explained in a preceding paragraph.

The special conception is sometimes characterized by the utmost perfectness of mechanical design. Here, however, is nothing to surprise us. The supreme wisdom which preordained the development of an idea in an insect's mind, might as easily as not have given it absolute perfectness. But—

3. Some animals have the power of modifying the special conception, when circumstances arise which prevent its being carried out in the usual way; and of realizing it in a great many different ways, on as many different occasions. And their work, on each of these occasions, is as perfect as in their carrying out the ordinary form of the conception. I beg leave to call the principle, by which they see thus how to shape their course so perfectly under new circumstances—intuition. To instance it, there is a beetle called the rhynchites betulæ. Its habit is, towards the end of May, to cut the leaves of the betula alba, or betula pubescens, into slips, which it rolls up into funnel-shaped chambers, which form singularly convenient cradles for its eggs. This is done after one pattern; and one may suppose it the mechanical realization of an inborn idea, as long as the leaf is perfect in shape. But if the leaf is imperfect, intuition steps upon the scene to aid the insect to cut its coat after its cloth. The sections made are then seen to vary with the varying shape of the leaf. Many different sections made by the insect were accurately drawn by a German naturalist, Dr. Debey. He submitted them for examination to Professor Heis of Aix-la-Chapelle. Upon

carefully studying them, Dr. Heis found these cuttings of the leaves, in suitableness to the end proposed, even to the minutest technical detail, to be in accordance with calculations compassable only through the higher mathematics, which, till modern times, were unknown to human intelligence. Such is the marvellous power of "intuition," displayed by certain insects. I know not how to define it but as a power of immediate reference to absolute truth, evinced by the insect in carrying out its little plans. It is evident that the insect uses the same power in realizing its ordinary special conception, when the result displays equal perfectness. And the question even crosses one's mind, Are the seemingly arbitrary plans really arbitrary?—may they not equally represent a highest type of design? But, be that as it may, the intuition of insects, as we now apprehend it, no longer stands an isolated phenomenon. The lucid cataleptic cannot less directly communicate with the source of truth, as she proves by foreseeing future events.

IV. The speculations of Berkeley and Boscovich on the non-existence of matter; and of Kant and others on the arbitrariness of all our notions, are interested in, for they appear to be refuted by, the intuitions of cataleptics. The cataleptic apprehends or perceives directly the objects around her; but they are the same as when realized through her senses. She notices no difference; size, form, colour, distance, are elements as real to her now as before. In respect again to the future, she sees it, but not in the sense of the annihilation of time; she foresees it; it is the future present to her; time she measures, present and future, with strange precision,—strange, yet an approximation, instead of this certainty, would have been still more puzzling.

So that it appears that our notions of matter, force, and the like, and of the conditions of space and time, apart from which we can conceive nothing, are not figments to suit our human and temporary being, but elements of eternal truth.

LETTER IX.

RELIGIOUS DELUSIONS—The seizures giving rise to them shown to have been forms of trance brought on by fanatical excitement—The Cevennes—Scenes at the tomb of the Abbé Paris—Revivals in America—The Ecstatica of Caldaro—Three forms of imputed demoniacal possession—Witchcraft; its marvels, and the solution.

THERE have been occasions, when much excitement on the subject of religion has prevailed, and when strange disorders of the nervous system have developed themselves among the people, which have been interpreted as immediate visitings of the Holy Spirit. The interpretation was delusive, the belief in it superstition. The effects displayed were neither more nor less than phenomena of trance, the physiological consequences of the prevailing excitement. The reader who has attentively perused the preceding letters will have no difficulty in identifying forms of this affection in the varieties of religious seizures, which, without further comment, I proceed to exemplify.

Every one will have met with allusions to some extraordinary scenes which took place in the Cevennes, at the close of the seventeenth century.

It was towards the end of the year 1688 that a report

was first heard of a gift of prophecy which had shown itself among the persecuted followers of the Reformation, who, in the south of France, had betaken themselves to the mountains. The first instance was said to have occurred in the family of a glass-dealer of the name of Du Serre, well known as the most zealous Calvinist of the neighbourhood, which was a solitary spot in Dauphiné, near Mount Peyra. In the enlarging circle of enthusiasts, Gabriel Astier and Isabella Vincent made themselves first conspicuous. Isabella, a girl of sixteen years of age, from Dauphiné, who was in the service of a peasant, and tended sheep, began in her sleep to preach and prophesy, and the Reformers came from far and near to hear her. An advocate of the name of Gerlan describes the following scene, which he had witnessed. At his request, she had admitted him and a good many others, after nightfall, to a meeting at a chateau in the neighbourhood. She there disposed herself upon a bed, shut her eyes, and went to sleep. In her sleep she chanted, in a low tone, the Commandments and a psalm. After a short respite she began to preach, in a louder voice—not in her own dialect, but in good French, which hitherto she had not used. The theme was an exhortation to obey God rather than man. Sometimes she spoke so quickly as to be hardly intelligible. At certain of her pauses she stopped to collect herself. She accompanied her words with gesticulations. Gerlan found her pulse quiet, her arm not rigid, but relaxed, as natural. After an interval, her countenance put on a mocking expression, and she began anew her exhortation, which was now mixed with ironical reflections upon the Church of Rome. She then suddenly stopped, continuing asleep. It was in vain they stirred her. When her arms were lifted and let go, they dropped unconsciously. As several now went away, whom her silence rendered impatient, she said in a low tone, but just as if she was awake,—"Why do you go away?—why do not you wait till I am ready?" And then she delivered another ironical discourse against the Catholic Church. She closed the scene with prayer.

When Bouchier, the intendant of the district, heard of the performances of Isabella Vincent, he had her brought before him. She replied to his interrogatories, that people had often told her that she preached in her sleep, but that she did not herself believe a word of it. As the slightness of her person made her appear younger than she really was, the intendant merely sent her to an hospital at Grenoble; where, notwithstanding that she was visited by persons of the Reformed persuasion, there was an end of her preaching—she became a Catholic!

Gabriel Astier, who had been a young labourer, likewise from Dauphiné, went, in the capacity of a preacher and prophet, into the valley of Bressac, in the Vivarais. He had infected his family: his father, mother, elder brother, and sweetheart, followed his example, and took to prophesying. Gabriel, before he preached, used to fall into a kind of stupor in which he lay rigid. After delivering his sermon, he would dismiss his auditors with a kiss, and the words—"My brother, or my sister, I impart to you the Holy Ghost." Many believed that they had thus received the Holy Ghost from Astier, being taken with the same seizure. During the period of the discourse, first one, then another, would fall down: some described themselves afterwards as having felt first a weakness and trembling through the whole frame, and an impulse to yawn and stretch their arms; then they fell, convulsed and foaming at the mouth. Others carried the contagion home with them, and first experienced its effects, days, weeks, or months afterwards. They believed —nor is it wonderful they did so—that they had received the Holy Ghost.

Not less curious were the seizures of the Convulsionnaires at the grave of the Abbé Paris, in the year 1727. These Jansenist visionaries used to collect in the churchyard of St. Médard, round the grave of the deposed and deceased deacon; and before long, the reputation of the place for working miracles getting about, they fell in troops into convulsions. They required, to gratify an internal impulse or feeling, that the most violent blows should be inflicted upon them at the pit of the stomach. Carré de Montgeron mentions that, being himself an enthusiast in the matter, he had inflicted the blows required with an iron instrument, weighing from twenty to thirty pounds, with a round head. And as a convulsionary lady complained that he struck too lightly to relieve the feeling of depression at her stomach, he gave her sixty blows with all his force. It would not do, and she begged to have the instrument used by a tall, strong man, who stood by in the crowd. The spasmodic tension of her muscles must have been enormous; for she received one hundred blows, delivered with such force that the wall shook behind her. She thanked the man for his benevolent aid, and contemptuously censured De Montgeron for his weakness, or want of faith, and timidity. It was, indeed, time for issuing the mandate, which, as wit read it, ran—

> "De par le roi—Défense à Dieu,
> De faire miracle en ce lieu."

In the revivals of modern times, scenes parallel to the above have been renewed.

"I have seen," says Mr. Le Roi Sunderland, himself a

preacher, (*Zion's Watchman*, New York, Oct. 2, 1842,) "persons often 'lose their strength,' as it is called, at camp-meetings and other places of great religious excitement; and not pious people alone, but those, also, who were not professors of religion. In the spring of 1824, while performing pastoral labour in Dennis, Massachusetts, I saw more than twenty affected in this way. Two young men, of the name of Crowell, came one day to a prayer-meeting. They were quite indifferent. I conversed with them freely, but they showed no signs of penitence. From the meeting they went to their shop, (they were shoemakers,) to finish some work before going to the meeting in the evening. On seating themselves, they were both struck perfectly stiff. I was immediately sent for, and found them sitting paralyzed" (he means taken with the initiatory form of trance-sleep, and possibly cataleptic) "on their benches, with their work in their hands, unable to get up, or to move at all. I have seen scores of persons affected the same way. I have seen persons lie in this state forty-eight hours. At such times they are unable to converse, and are sometimes unconscious of what is passing round them. At the same time, they say they are in a happy state of mind."

The following extract from the same journal portrays another kind of nervous seizure, as it was manifested at the great revival some forty years ago, at Kentucky and Tennessee.

"The convulsions were commonly called 'the jerks.' A writer, (M'Neman) quoted by Mr. Power, (*Essay on the Influence of the Imagination over the Nervous System,*) gives this account of their course and progress:

"'At first appearance these meetings exhibited nothing to the spectator but a scene of confusion that could scarcely be put into language. They were generally opened with a sermon, near the close of which there would be an unusual outcry, some bursting out into loud ejaculations of prayer, &c.

"'The rolling exercise consisted in being cast down in a violent manner, doubled with the head and feet together, or stretched in a prostrate manner, turning swiftly over like a dog. Nothing in nature could better represent the jerks, than for one to goad another alternately on every side with a piece of red-hot iron. The exercise commonly began in the head, which would fly backwards and forwards, and from side to side, with a quick jolt, which the person would naturally labour to suppress, but in vain. He must necessarily go on as he was stimulated, whether with a violent dash on the ground, and bounce from place to place, like a foot-ball; or hopping round, with head, limbs, and trunk twitching and jolting in every direction, as if they must inevitably fly asunder,'" &c.

The following sketch is from Dow's journal. In the year 1805 he preached at Knoxville, Tennessee, before the governor, when some hundred and fifty persons, among whom were a number of Quakers, had the jerks. "I have seen," says the writer, "all denominations of religion exercised by the jerks—gentleman and lady, black and white, young and old, without exception. I passed a meeting-house, where I observed the undergrowth had been cut down for camp-meetings, and from fifty to a hundred saplings were left for the people who were jerked to hold by. I observed where they had held on they had kicked up the earth, as a horse stamping flies."

A widely different picture to the above is given in a letter from the Earl of Shrewsbury to A. M. Phillips,

Esq., published in 1841, and describing the state of two *religieuses*, (the Ecstatica of Caldaro, and the Addolorata of Capriana,) who were visited by members of their own communion, in the belief that they lay in a sort of heavenly beatitude. To this idea their stillness, the devotional attitude of their hands and expression of their countenances, together with their manifestation of miraculous intuition, contributed. But I am afraid that, to the eye of a physician, their condition would have been simple trance. However, while the absence of reasonable enlightenment in the display is to be regretted, one agreeably recognises the influence of the humanity of modern times. Had these young women lived two centuries ago, they would have been the subjects of other discipline, and their history, had I possessed it to quote, must have been transferred to the darker section which I have next to enter on.

The belief in possession by devils, which existed in the middle ages and subsequently, embraced several dissimilar cases. The first of them which I will exemplify would have included individuals in the state of the *religieuses* described by Lord Shrewsbury. Behaviour and powers which the people could not understand, even if exhibited by good and virtuous persons, and only expressive of or used for right purposes, were construed into the operation of unholy influences. The times were the reign of terror in religion. I give the following instance:—Marie Bucaille, a native of Normandy, became, towards the year 1700, the subject of fits, which ordinarily lasted three or four hours. It appears, by the depositions of persons of character on her trial, that Marie had effected many cures seemingly by her prayers; that she comprehended and executed directions given to her mentally;

that she read the thoughts of others. When in the fit, the Curé of Golleville placed in the hands of Marie a folded note. Without opening the note, she replied to the questions which it contained; and, without knowing the writer, she accurately described her person. Although Marie only employed her powers to cure the sick and in the service of religion, she was not the less condemned to death by the parliament of Valogne. The parliament of Rouen mitigated her punishment to whipping and public ignominy.

A second class, who came nearer to the exact idea of being possessed by devils, were persons who were deranged, and entertained something of that impression themselves, and avowed it. I am not speaking of single instances, but of an extensive popular delusion, or frenzy rather, which prevailed in the fifteenth and sixteenth centuries in parts of Europe as an epidemic seizure. It was called the wolf-sickness. Those affected betook themselves to the forests as wild beasts. One of these, who was brought before De Lancre, at Bordeaux, in the beginning of the sixteenth century, was a young man of Besançon. He avowed himself to be huntsman of the forest lord, his invisible master. He believed that, through the power of his master, he had been transformed into a wolf; that he hunted in the forest as such; and that he was often accompanied by a bigger wolf, whom he suspected to be the master he served; with more details of the same kind. The persons thus affected were called Wehrwolves. Their common fate was the alternative of recovering from their derangement, under the influence of exorcism and its accessories, or of being executed.

The third and proper type of possession by devils presented more complicated features. The patient's state was not uniform. Often, or for the most part, his appearance and behaviour were natural; then paroxysms would supervene, in which he appeared fierce, malignant, demoniacal, in which he believed himself to be possessed, and acted up to the character, and in which powers, seemingly superhuman, such as reading the thoughts of others, were manifested by the possessed. The explanation of these features is happily given by Dr. Fischer of Basle, author of an excellent work on Somnambulism. He resolves them, with evident justice, into recurrent fits of trance—the patient, when entranced, being at the same time deranged; and he exemplifies his hypothesis by the case of a German lady who had fits of trance, in which she fancied herself a French emigrée: it would have been as easy for her, had it been the mode, to have fancied herself, and to have played the part of being, possessed by the fiend. The case is this:

Gmelin, in the first volume of his *Contributions to Anthropology*, narrates that, in the year 1789, a German lady, under his observation, had daily paroxysms, in which she believed herself to be, and acted the part of, a French Emigrant. She had been in distress of mind through the absence of a person she was attached to, and he was somehow implicated in the scenes of the French Revolution. After an attack of fever and delirium, the complaint regulated itself, and took the form of a daily fit of trance-waking. When the time for the fit approached, she stopped in her conversation, and ceased to answer when spoken to; she then remained a few minutes sitting perfectly still, her eyes fixed on the carpet before her. Then, in evident uneasiness, she began to move her head backwards and forwards, to sigh and to pass her fingers across her eyebrows. This lasted a minute; then she raised her eyes, looked once or twice round with timidity and embarrassment, then began to talk in French, when she would describe all the particulars of her escape from France, and, assuming the manner of a French woman, talk purer and better accented French than she had been known to be capable of talking before, correct her friends when they spoke incorrectly, but delicately, and with a comment on the German rudeness of laughing at the bad pronunciation of strangers: and if led herself to speak or read German, she used a French accent, and spoke it ill; and the like.

We have by this time had intercourse enough with spirits and demons to prepare us for the final subject of witchcraft.

The superstition of witchcraft stretches back into remote antiquity, and has many roots. In Europe it is partly of Druidical origin. The Druidesses were part priestesses, part shrewd old ladies, who dealt in magic and medicine. They were called *allrune*, all-knowing. There was some touch of classical superstition mingled in the stream which was flowing down to us; so an edict of a Council of Trêves, in the year 1310, has this injunction:—"Nulla mulierum se nocturnis horis equitare cum Dianâ profiteatur; hæc enim dæmoniaca est illusio." But the main source from which we derived this superstition is the East, and traditions and facts incorporated in our religion. There were only wanted the ferment of thought of the fifteenth century, the energy, ignorance, enthusiasm, and faith of those days, and the papal denunciation of witchcraft by the Bull of Innocent the Eighth, in 1459, to give fury to the delusion. And from this time, for three centuries, the flames at which more than a hundred thousand victims perished cast a lurid light over Europe.

But the fires are out—the superstition is extinct—and its history is trite, and has lost all interest; so I will hasten to the one point in it which deserves, which indeed requires, explanation.

I do not advert to the late duration of the belief in witchcraft—so late, that it is but a century this very month of January since the last witch, a lady and a sub-prioress, whose confession I will afterwards give, was executed in Germany; while, at the same period, a strong effort was made in Scotland, by good and conscientious, and otherwise sensible persons, to reanimate the embers of the delusion, as is shown by the following evidence. In February, 1743, the Associate Presbytery, meaning the Presbytery of the Secession or Seceders, (from the Scottish Established Church,) passed, and soon thereafter published, an act for renewing the National Covenant, in which there is a solemn acknowledgment of sins, and vow to renounce them; among which sins is specified "the repeal of the penal statutes against witchcraft, contrary to the express laws of God, and for which a holy God may be provoked, in a way of righteous judgment, to leave those who are already ensnared to be hardened more and more, and to permit Satan to tempt and seduce others to the same wicked and dangerous snare."—(Note, *Edinburgh Review*, January, 1847.)

Nor is the marvel in the absolute belief of the people in witchcraft only two centuries ago: what could they do but believe, when the witches and sorcerers themselves, before their execution, often avowed their guilt and told how they had laid themselves out to league with the evil spirit; how they had gone through a regular process of initiation in the black art; how they had been rebaptized with the support of regular witch-sponsors; how they had abjured Christ, and had entered, to the best of their belief, into a compact with the Devil, and had commenced accordingly a suitable course of bad works, poisoning and bewitching men and cattle, and the like?

Nor is the wonder in the unfairness with which those accused of witchcraft were treated. So at Lindheim, Horst reports on one occasion six women were implicated in a charge of having disinterred the body of a child to make a witchbroth. As they happened to be innocent of the deed, they underwent the most cruel tortures before they would confess it. At length they saw their cheapest bargain was to admit the crime, and be simply burned alive, and have it over. They did so. But the husband of one of them procured an official examination of the grave, when the child's body was found in its coffin safe and sound. What said the Inquisitor? "This is indeed a proper piece of devil's work: no, no, I am not to be taken in by such a gross and obvious imposture. Luckily the women have already confessed the crime, and burned they must and shall be, in honour of the Holy Trinity, which has commanded the extirpation of sorcerers and witches." The six women were burned alive accordingly; for the people had fits of frenzied terror, which required to be allayed by the sacrifice of a victim or two, and Justice became confused: to be sure, in those days her head was never very clear, and threw by mistake the odium of the crime into the accusing scale; the other flew up significantly of the full extent to which mercy could interfere to temper the law. A curious instance of an epidemic attack of the belief in witchcraft occurred at Salzburg between the years 1627 and 1629, originating in a sickness among the cattle in the neighbourhood. The sickness was unluckily attributed to witchcraft, and an active inquiry was set on foot to detect the participators in the crime. It was very successful; for we find in the list of persons burned alive on this occasion, besides children of 14, 12, 11, 10, 9 years of age, fourteen canons, four gentlemen of the choir, two young men of rank, a fat old lady of rank, the wife of a burgomaster, a counsellor, the fattest burgess of Würtzburg, together with his wife, the handsomest woman in the city, and a midwife of the name of Shiekelte, with whom (according to a N. B. in the original report) the whole of the mischief originated.

The marvel in witchcraft is the belief entertained by the sorcerers and witches themselves of its reality. That many of these persons, shrewd and unprincipled, should have pretended an implicit belief in their art, till they were brought to justice, is only what is still occasionally done in modern times. But that they should, as it is proved by some of their confessions previous to execution, have been their own dupes, and have entertained no doubt whatsoever of the reality of their intercourse with the devil, is surprising enough to deserve explanation. A single crucial instance will bring us upon the trail of the solution.

A little maid, twelve years of age, used to fall into fits of sleep; and afterwards she told her parents and the judge how an old woman and her daughter, riding on a broomstick, had come and taken her out with them. The daughter sat foremost, the old woman behind, the little maid between. They went away through the roof of the house, over the adjoining houses and the towngate, to a village some way off. Upon arriving there, the party went down the chimney of a cottage into a room, where sat a black man and twelve women. They eat and drank. The black man filled their glasses from a can, and gave each of the women a handful of gold. She herself had received none, but she had eaten and drunk with them.

See how much this example displays. I mean not that the superstition was imbibed in childhood, though that would do much to establish the belief in it, but that it had power to disturb the mind sufficiently to produce trance-sleep; for such were evidently the fits of sleep this child described; and trance-sleep, with its special character of visions, of dreams vivid, coherent, continuous, realizing the ideas which had driven the mind into trance. Elder persons, it is to be presumed, were occasionally similarly wrought upon. And the witches seemed to have known and availed themselves of the confidence in their art that could be thus promoted; and by witch-broths, of which narcotics formed an ingredient, they would induce in themselves and in their pupils a heavy stupor, which so far resembles trance that vivid and connected dreams occur in it. Here was the seeming reality necessary for absolute belief. It lay in not understood trance-phenomena. Other evidence from the same source came in to support the first. Some of the witch-pupils in their trances would show a strange knowledge; some of the victims, on whose fears or persons they had wrought, would become possessed—proving their art to be not less real than they believed thus the elementary part to be of their personal communication with the fiend. These remarks explain collaterally why witches and sorceresses were more numerous than sorcerers and magicians. Insufficient occupation and other causes helped probably to dispose women to seek a resource in the intense excitement of this crime; but besides, trance stood at their service, which men seldomer experience.

I will conclude with two pictures. One, the confession—interesting, however, from its relation to the child's early vision—of vulgar and ordinary witches; the other, the substance of the confession of a lady-witch, which, in itself, tells the whole curious tale of this disease.

At Mora, in Sweden, in 1669, of many who were put to the torture and executed, seventy-two women agreed in the following avowal: That they were in the habit of meeting at a place called Blocula. That on their calling out "Come forth," the Devil used to appear to them in a gray coat, red breeches, gray stockings, with a red beard, and a peaked hat with parti-coloured feathers on his head. He then enforced upon them, not without blows, that they must bring him, at nights, their own and other people's children, stolen for the purpose. They travel through the air to Blocula either on beasts, or on spits, or broomsticks. When they have many children with them, they rig on an additional spar to lengthen the back of the goat or their broomstick, that the children may have room to sit. At Blocula they sign their name in blood, and are baptized. The Devil is a humorous, pleasant gentleman; but his table is coarse enough, which makes the children often sick on their way home, the product being the so-called witch-butter found in the fields. When the Devil is larky, he solicits the witches to dance round him on their brooms, which he suddenly pulls from under them, and uses to beat them with, till they are black and blue. He laughs at this joke till his sides shake again. Sometimes he is in a more gracious mood, and plays to them lovely airs upon the harp; and occasionally sons and daughters are born to the Devil, which take up their residence at Blocula.

The following is the history of the lady-witch. She

was, at the time of her death, seventy years of age, and had been many years sub-prioress of the convent of Unterzell, near Würtzburg.

Maria Renata took the veil at nineteen years of age, against her inclination, having previously been initiated in the mysteries of witchcraft, which she continued to practise for fifty years, under the cloak of punctual attendance to discipline and pretended piety. She was long in the station of sub-prioress, and would, for her capacity, have been promoted to the rank of prioress, had she not betrayed a certain discontent with the ecclesiastical life, a certain contrariety to her superiors, something half expressed only of inward dissatisfaction. Renata had not ventured to let any one about the convent into her confidence, and she remained free from suspicion, notwithstanding that, from time to time, some of the nuns, either from the herbs she mixed with their food, or through sympathy, had strange seizures, of which some died. Renata became at length extravagant and unguarded in her witch-propensities, partly from long security, partly from desire of stronger excitement—made noises in the dormitory, and uttered shrieks in the garden; went at nights into the cells of the nuns to pinch and torment them, to assist her in which she kept a considerable supply of cats. The removal of the keys of the cells counteracted this annoyance; but a still more efficient means was a determined blow, on the part of a nun, struck at the aggressor with the penitential scourge one night, on the morning following which Renata was observed to have a black eye and cut face. This event awakened suspicion against Renata. Then one of the nuns, who was much esteemed, declared, believing herself upon her death-bed, that, "as she shortly expected to stand before her Maker,

Renata was uncanny; that she had often at nights been visibly tormented by her, and that she warned her to desist from this course." General alarm arose, and apprehension of Renata's arts; and one of the nuns, who previously had had fits, now became possessed, and, in the paroxysms, told the wildest tales against Renata. It is only wonderful how the sub-prioress contrived to keep her ground so many years against these suspicions and incriminations. She adroitly put aside the insinuations of the nun as imaginary, or of calumnious intention, and treated witchcraft and possession of the Devil as things which enlightened people no longer believed in. As, however, five more of the nuns, either taking the infection from the first, or influenced by the arts of Renata, became possessed of devils, and unanimously attacked Renata, the superiors could no longer avoid making a serious investigation of the charges. Renata was confined to a cell alone, whereupon the six devils screeched in chorus at being deprived of their friend. She had begged to be allowed to take her papers with her; but this being refused, and thinking herself detected, she at once avowed to her confessor and the superiors that she was a witch, had learned witchcraft out of the convent, and had bewitched the six nuns. They determined to keep the matter secret, and to attempt the conversion of Renata. And, as the nuns still continued possessed, they despatched her to a remote convent. Here, under a show of outward piety, she still went on with her attempts to realize witchcraft, and the nuns remained possessed. It was decided at length to give Renata over to the civil power. She was accordingly condemned to be burned alive; but in mitigation of punishment, her head was first struck off. Four of the possessed nuns gradually recovered, with clerical assistance—the other two remained deranged. Renata was executed on the 21st January, 1749.

Renata stated, in her voluntary confession, that she had often, at night, been carried bodily to witch-sabbaths, in one of which she was first presented to the Prince of Darkness, when she abjured God and the Virgin at the same time. Her name, with the alteration of Maria into Emma, was written in a black book, and she herself was stamped on the back as the Devil's property; in return for which she received the promise of seventy years of life, and of all she might wish for. She stated that she had often at night gone into the cellar of the chateau and drank the best wine; in the shape of a sow had walked on the convent walls; on the bridge had milked the cows as they passed over; and several times had mingled with the actors in the theatre in London.

LETTER X.

MESMERISM.—Use of chloroform—History of Mesmer—The true nature and extent of his discovery—Its applications to medicine and surgery—Various effects produced by mesmeric manipulations—Hysteric seizures—St. Veitz's dance—Nervous paralysis—Catochus—Initiatory trance—The order in which the higher trance phenomena are afterwards generally drawn out.

CAN no further use be made of the facts and principles we have thus seen verified and established, than to explain a class of delusions which prevailed in times of ignorance? The powers which we have seen successfully employed to shake the nerves and unsettle the mind in the service of superstition, can they not be skilfully turned to some purpose beneficial to society?

A satisfactory answer to the question may be found in the invention of ether-inhalation, and in the history of mesmerism. The witch narcotized her pupils in order to produce in them delusive visions; the surgeon stupefies his patient to annul the pain of an operation. The fanatic preacher excites convulsions and trance in his auditory as evidence of the working of the Holy Spirit; Mesmer produced the same effects in his patients as a means of curing disease.

It occurred to Mr. Jackson, a chemist of the United States, that it might be possible harmlessly to stupefy a patient through the inhalation of the vapour of sulphuric ether, to such an extent that a surgical operation would be unfelt by him. He communicated the idea to Mr. Morton, a dentist, who carried it into execution with the happiest results. The patient became insensible; a tooth was extracted; no pain seemed felt at the time, or was remembered afterwards, and no ill consequences followed. Led by the report of this success, in the course of the autumn of 1846, Messrs. Bigelow, Warren, and Heywood, ventured to employ the same means in surgical operations of a more serious description. The results obtained on these occasions were not less satisfactory than the first had been. Since then, in England, France, and Germany, the same interesting experiment has been repeated many hundred times, and the adoption of this, or of a parallel method, has become general in surgery.

I withdraw from the present Letter a sketch which I had made from the "report" of Dr. Heyfelder, of the phenomena of etherization; for a year had barely elapsed, when the narcotizing agent recommended by Mr. Jackson was superseded by another, suggested and brought into use by Professor Simpson of Edinburgh. The inhalation of chloroform is found to be more rapid, uniform, and certain in its effects, and compassable in a simpler manner, than the inhalation of ether. Its brief phenomena are wound up by the production of stupor; they are remotely comparable to those produced by alcohol. Alas! the time is passed when I enjoyed the means of looking through, and forming a practical judgment upon discoveries like the present. Not the less, however, do I hail the advent of this as a boon to the art of surgery. The conception was original, bold and reasonable; its execution neat and scientific; its success wonderful. It established in the year 1847, to the satisfaction of the public and of the medical profession, that the exclusion of pain from surgical operations is a practicable idea, and the attempt to realise it a legitimate pursuit.

Then, what is Mesmerism?

The object of the inventor of the art was to cure diseases through the influence of a new force brought by him to bear upon the human frame.

Talent, for philosophy or business, is the power of seeing what is yet hidden from others. As the eyes of some animals are fitted to see best in the dark, so the mental vision of some original minds prefers exercising itself on obscure and occult subjects. Whoever indulges this turn will certainly pass for a charlatan; most likely he will prove one. Mesmer had it, and indulged it, in a high degree. The body of science which I have unfolded in the preceding Letters was wholly unknown in his time, (he was born in 1734;) but he was led by his wayward instinct to grope after it in the dark, and he seized and brought to upper light fragmentary elements of strange capabilities, which he strove to interpret and to use. He had early displayed a bias towards the mystical. When a student at Vienna, (he was by birth a Swiss,) his principal study was astrology. He sought in the stars a force which, extending throughout space, might influence the beings living upon our planet. In the year 1766 he published his lucubrations. In attempting to identify his imaginary force, Mesmer first supposed it to be electricity. Afterwards, about the year 1773, he adopted the idea that it must be magnetism. So at Vienna, from 1773 to 1775, he employed the practice of stroking diseased parts of the body with magnets. But in 1776, happening to be upon a tour, he fell in with a mystical monk of the name of Gassner, who was then occupied in curing the Prince-Bishop of Ratisbon of blindness, by exorcism. Then Mesmer observed that, without magnets, Gassner produced much the same effects on the living body which he had produced with them. The fact was not lost upon him: he threw aside his magnets, and operated mostly afterwards with the hand alone. It appears that he was often successful in curing disease, or that his patients not only experienced sensible effects from his procedures, but frequently recovered from their complaints. But in 1777, his reputation, which must have always hung upon a very slender thread, broke down through a failure in the case of the musician Paradies. So Mesmer left Vienna, and in the following year betook himself to Paris. There he obtained a success which quickly drew upon him the indignation, perhaps the jealousy, of the Faculty, who failed not to stigmatize him as a charlatan. They exclaimed against him for practising an art which he would not divulge; and when he offered to display it, averred that he threw difficulties in the way of their investigations. Perhaps he suspected them of want of fairness in their inquiries; perhaps he was really unwilling to part with his secret. He refused an offer from the Government of 20,000 francs if he would disclose it; but he communicated freely to individuals, under a pledge of secrecy, all he knew for a hundred louis. His practice itself gave most support to the allegations against him. His patients were received with an air of mystery and studied effect. The apartment, hung with mirrors, was dimly lighted. A profound silence was observed, broken only by strains of music, which occasionally floated through the rooms. The patients were seated round a sort of vat, which contained a heterogeneous mixture of chemical ingredients. With this, and with each other, they were placed in relation by means of cords, or jointed rods, or by holding hands; and among them slowly and mysteriously moved Mesmer himself, affecting one by a touch, another by a look, a third by passes with his hand, a fourth by pointing with a rod.

What followed is easily conceivable from the scenes referred to in my last letter as witnessed at religious revivals. One person became hysterical, then another; one was seized with catalepsy; others with convulsions; some with palpitations of the heart, perspirations, and other bodily disturbances. These effects, however various and different, went all by the name of "salutary crisis." The method was supposed to provoke in the sick person exactly the kind of action propitious to his recovery. And it may easily be imagined that many a patient found himself the better after a course of this rude empiricism, and that the effect made by these events passing daily in Paris must have been very considerable. To the ignorant the scene was full of wonderment.

To ourselves, regarding it from our present vantage-ground, it presents no marvellous characters. The phenomena were the same which we have been recently contemplating—a group of disorders of the nervous system. The causes which were present are not less familiar to us, nor their capability of producing such effects; they were—mental excitement, here consisting in raised expectation and fear; the contagiousness of hysteria, convulsions, and trance, its force increased by the numbers and close-packing of the patients; the Od force, developed by the chemical action in the charged caldron, developed by each of the excited bodies around, its action first favoured by the absolute stillness observed, then by the increasing sensibility of the patients as their nerves became more and more shaken. It is remarkable that Jussieu—the most competent judge in the commission of inquiry into the truth of mesmerism, set on foot at Paris in 1784, of which Franklin was a member, and which condemned mesmerism as an imposture—was so struck with what he saw, that he strongly recommended the subject to the attention and study of physicians. His objections were against the theory alone. He laid it down in the separate report which he gave in, that no physical cause had been proved to be in operation beyond animal heat! curiously overlooking the fact that common heat would not produce the effects observed; and, therefore, that the latter must have been owing to that something which animal heat, or the radiating warmth of a living body, contains, in addition to common heat. That something we now know, but only since 1845, to be the Od force.

The Od force is so new, so young in science, that Mesmer's reputation has not yet been credited with the honour thence reflected upon it. I will not say that Mesmer's astral force was a distinct anticipation of Von Reichenbach's discovery, which was noways suggested by the former, and was from first to last an effort of inductive observation. But the guess of the mystic had certainly a most happy parallelism to the truth, which a different sort of mind tracked in the same field; for the Od force reaches us even from the stars, and the sun and the fixed stars are Od-negative; and the planets and the moon Od-positive. It is unnecessary to follow Mesmer through his minor performances. The relief sometimes obtained by stroking diseased parts with the hand—that is, the effects obtained through the local action of Od—had been before proclaimed by Dr. Greatrex, whose pretensions had had no less an advocate than the Honourable Robert Boyle. The extraordinary tales of Mesmer's personal power over individuals are probably part exaggeration, part real results of his confidence and skill in the use of the means he wielded. Mesmer died in 1815.

Among his pupils, when at the zenith of his fame, was the Marquis de Puységur. Returning from serving at the siege of Gibraltar, this young officer found mesmerism the mode at Paris, and appears to have become, for no other reason, one of the initiated. At the end of a course of instruction, he professed himself to be no wiser than when it began; and he ridiculed the credulity of his brothers, who were stanch adherents of the new doctrine. However, he did not forget his lesson; and on going the same spring to his estate at Besancy, near Soissons, he took occasion to mesmerize the daughter of his agent and another young person, for the toothache, and they declared themselves, in a few minutes, cured. This questionable success was sufficient to lead M. de Puységur, a few days after, to try his hand on a young peasant of the name of Victor, who was suffering with a severe fluxion on his chest. What was M. de Puységur's surprise, when, at the end of a few minutes, Victor went off into a kind of tranquil sleep, without crisis or convulsion, and in that sleep began to gesticulate and talk, and enter into his private affairs. Then he became sad; and M. de Puységur tried mentally to inspire him with cheerful thoughts; he hummed a lively tune to himself inaudibly, and immediately Victor began to sing the air. Victor remained asleep for an hour, and awoke composed, with his symptoms mitigated.

The case of Victor revolutionized the art of mesmerism. The large part of his life, in which M. de Puységur had nothing to do but to follow this vein of inquiry, was occupied in practising and advocating a gentle manipulation to produce sleep, in preference to the more exciting means which led to the violent crises in Mesmer's art. I have no plea for telling how M. de Puységur served in the first French revolutionary armies; how he quitted the service in disgust; how narrowly he escaped the guillotine; how he lived in retirement afterwards, benevolently endeavouring to do good to his sick neighbours by means of mesmerism; how he survived the Restoration; and how, finally, he died of a cold caught by serving in the encampment at Rheims, at the coronation of Charles X.

For he had fulfilled his mission the day that he put Victor to sleep. He had made a vast stride in advance of his teacher. Not but that Mesmer must frequently have induced the same condition; but he had passed it by unheeded as one only of numerous equivalent forms of salutary crises; or that M. de Puységur himself estimated, or had the means of estimating, the real nature and value of the step which he had made. To himself he appeared to be winning a larger domain for mesmerism, when in fact he had emerged into an independent field, into which mesmerism happened to have a gate.

The state which he had induced in Victor was common trance, the initiatory sleep, followed by half-waking. He had obtained this result by using the Od force with quietness and gentleness, leaving out the exciting mental agencies to which the mixture of violent seizures in Mesmer's practice is attributable. The gentler method has been adopted and practised by the successors of M. de Puységur, by Deleuze, Bertrand, Georget, Rostan, Foissac, Elliotson, and others. To Dr. Elliotson, the most successful probably, certainly the most scientific employer of the practice of mesmerism, the credit is due of having introduced its use into England: the credit,—for it required no little moral courage to encounter the storm of opposition with which his honest zeal in the advocacy of an unpopular practical truth was met. It is but fair to add, that though his theory has been superseded, and his method changed, to Mesmer belongs the merit of having first tracked out and realized this path of discovery. The golden medal is his.

The modern practice of mesmerism contemplates two objects: one, the application of the Od force to produce local effects; the other, its employment to induce trance. In the present slight sketch I shall say nothing on the first subject; but let me describe how trance is induced. It is to be observed, that attention to certain conditions favours very much the success of the experiment. The room should not be too light; very few persons should be present; the patient and the operator should be quiet, tranquil, and composed; the patient should be fasting.

The operator has then only to sit down before the patient, who is likewise sitting with his hands resting on his knees, and gently closed, with the thumbs upwards. The operator then lays his hands half-open upon the patient's, pressing the thumbs against those of the patient, as it were taking thumbs: this is a more convenient attitude than taking hands in the ordinary way. The operator and patient have then only to sit still. An Od-current is established; and if the patient is susceptible, he will soon become drowsy, and perhaps be entranced at the first sitting. Instead of this, the two hands of the operator may be held horizontally with the fingers pointed to the patient's forehead, and either maintained in this position, or brought downwards in frequent passes opposite to the patient's face, shoulders, arms; the points of the fingers being held as near the patient as possible without touching.

It is easy, theoretically, to explain the beneficial results which follow from the daily induction of trance for an hour or so, in various forms of disorder of the nervous system,—in epilepsy,—in tic-doloreux,—in nervous palsy, and the like. As long as the state of trance is maintained, so long is the nervous system in a state of repose. It is more or less completely put out of gear. It experiences the same relief which a sprained joint feels when you dispose it in a relaxed position on a pillow. A chance is thus given to the strained nerves of recovering their tone of health; and it is wonderful how many cases of nervous disorder get well at once through these simple means. As it is certain that there is no disease in which the nervous system is not primarily or secondarily implicated, it is impossible to foresee what will prove the limit to the beneficial application of mesmerism in medical practice.

In operative surgery the art is not less available. In trance the patient is insensible, and a limb may be removed without the operation exciting disturbance of any kind. And what is equally important, in all the after-treatment, at every dressing, the process of mesmerizing may be resorted to again, with no possible disadvantage, but being rather soothing and useful to the patient, independently of the extinction of the dread and suffering of pain. The first instance in which an operation was performed on a patient in this state was the celebrated case of Madame Plantin. It occurred twenty years ago. The lady was sixty-four years of age, and laboured under scirrhus of the breast. She was prepared for the operation by M. Chapélain, who on several successive days threw her into trance by the ordinary mesmeric manipulations. She was *then* like an ordinary sleep-walker, and would converse with indifference about the contemplated operation, the idea of which, when she was in her natural state, filled her with terror. The operation of removing the diseased breast was performed at Paris on the 12th of April, 1829, by M. Jules Cloquet; it lasted from ten to twelve minutes. During the whole of this time the patient, *in her trance*, conversed calmly with M. Cloquet, and exhibited not the slightest sign of suffering. Her expression of countenance did not change; nor was the voice, the breathing, or the pulse at all affected. After the wound was dressed, the patient was awakened from the trance, when on learning that the operation was over, and seeing her children round her, Madame Plantin was affected with considerable emotion, whereupon M. Chapélain, to compose her, put her back into the state of trance.

I copy the above particulars from Dr. Foissac's *Rap-*

ports et Discussions de l'Académie Royale de Médecine sur le Magnetism Animal.—Paris, 1833. My friend, Dr. Warren, of Boston, informed me that, being at Paris, he had asked M. Jules Cloquet if the story were true. M. Cloquet answered, "Perfectly." "Then why," said Dr. Warren, "have you not repeated the practice?" M. Cloquet replied "that he had not dared; that the prejudice against mesmerism was so strong at Paris that he probably would have lost his reputation and his income by so doing."

It has been mentioned that in ordinary trance the mind appears to gain new powers. For a long time we had to trust to the chance turning up of cases of spontaneous trance, in the experience of physicians of observation, for any light we could hope would be thrown on those extraordinary phenomena; now we possess around us, on every side, adequate opportunities for completely elucidating these events, if we please to employ them. The philosopher, when his speculations suggest a new question to be put, can summon the attendance of a trance as easily as the Jupiter of the Iliad summoned a dream; or, looking out for two or three cases to which the induction of trance may be beneficial, the physician may have in his house subjects for perpetual reference and daily experiment.

A gentleman, with whom I have long been well acquainted, for many years chairman of the Quarter Sessions in a northern county, of which during a late year he was high sheriff, has, like M. de Puységur, amused some of his leisure hours, and benevolently done not a little good, by taking the trouble of mesmerizing invalids, whom he has thus restored to health. In constant correspondence with, and occasionally having the pleasure of seeing this gentleman, I have learned from him the common course in which the new powers of the mind, which belong to trance, are developed under its artificial induction. The sketch which I propose to give of this subject will be taken from his descriptions, which, I should observe, tally in all essential points with what I meet with in French and German authors. The little that I have myself seen of the matter, I will mention preliminarily.

In some, instead of trance, a common fit of hysterics is produced; in others, slight headache, and a sense of weight on the eyebrows, and difficulty of raising the eyelids, supervene.

In one young woman, whom I saw mesmerised for the first time by Dupotet, nothing resulted but a sense of pricking and tingling wherever he pointed with his hand; and her arm, on one or two occasions, jumped in the most natural and conclusive manner when, her eyes being covered, he directed his outstretched finger to it.

A gentleman, about thirty years of age, when the mesmeriser held his outstretched hands pointed to his head, experienced no disposition to sleep; but in two or three minutes he began to shake his head and twist his features about; at last, his head was jerked from side to side, and forwards and backwards, with a violence that looked alarming. But he said, when it was over, that the motion had not been unpleasant; that he had moved in a sort voluntarily—although he could not refrain from it. If the hands of the operator were pointed to his arm instead of his head, the same violent jerks ensued, and gradually extended to the whole body. I asked him to try to resist the influence, by holding his arm out in strong muscular tension. This had the effect of retarding the attack of the jerks, but, when it came on, it was more violent than usual. I have lately seen another similar case. The seizure is evidently a form of St. Veitz's dance brought out by the operation of the Od force. In neither of these two cases could trance be induced.

A servant of mine, aged about twenty-five, was mesmerized by Lafontaine, for a full half-hour, and, no effect appearing to be produced, I told him he might rise from the chair and leave us. On getting up he looked uneasy, and said his arms were numb. They were perfectly paralyzed from the elbows downwards, and numb to the shoulders. This was the more satisfactory, that neither the man himself, nor Lafontaine, nor the four or five spectators, expected this result. The operator triumphantly drew a pin and stuck it into the man's hand, which bled, but had no feeling. Then heedlessly, to show it gave pain, Lafontaine stuck the pin into the man's thigh, whose flashing eye, and half suppressed growl, denoted that the aggression would certainly have been returned by another, had the arm which should have done it not been really powerless. However, M. Lafontaine made peace with the man, by restoring him the use and feeling of his arms. This was done by dusting them, as it were, by quick transverse motions of his extended hands. In five minutes nothing remained of the palsy but a slight stiffness, which gradually wore off in the course of the evening.

Occasionally partial tonic spasm (improperly termed catalepsy, for it is of the nature of catochus, and the rigidity attending it is absolute) supervenes as the only consequence of mesmerising a limb. This result, which is not less alarming to the patient who has not been led to expect it than the preceding, may be got rid of in the same way. If you point with your fingers to the rigid muscles, or again, as it were, dust the limb with brisk transverse passes, or breathe upon it, the stiffness is thawed and disappears. Trance is seldom induced by mesmeric passes without more or less partial muscular rigidity of this kind supervening; it always yields to the means which have been mentioned.

Genuine and ordinary trance I have seen produced by the same manipulations in from three minutes to half-an-hour. The patient's eyelids have dropped, he has appeared on the point of sleeping, but he has not sunk back upon his chair; then he has continued to sit upright—seemingly perfectly insensible to the loudest sounds, or the acutest and most startling impressions on the sense of touch. The pulse is commonly a little increased in frequency; the breathing is sometimes heavier than usual.

Occasionally, as in Victor's case, the patient quickly and spontaneously emerges from the state of trance-sleep into trance half-waking—a rapidity of development which I am persuaded occurs much more frequently among the French than with the English or Germans. English patients, especially, for the most part require a long course of education, many sittings, to have the same powers drawn out. And these are by far the most interesting cases. I will describe, from Mr. Williamson's account, the course he has usually followed in developing his patient's powers, and the order in which they have manifested themselves.

On the first day, perhaps, nothing can be elicited. But after some minutes, the stupor seems, as it were, less embarrassing to the patient, who appears less heavily slumbrous, and breathes lighter again: or it may be the reverse, particularly if the patient is epileptic; after a little, the breathing may be deeper, the state one of less composure. Pointing with the hands to the pit of the stomach, laying the hands upon the shoulders, and slowly moving them along the arms down to the hands, the whole with the utmost quietude and composure on the part of the operator, will dispel this oppression.

And the interest of the first sitting is confined to the process of awakening the patient, which is one of the most marvellous phenomena of the whole. The operator lays his two thumbs on the space between the eyebrows, and as it were vigorously smooths or irons the eyebrows, rubbing them from within outwards seven or eight times. Upon this, the patient probably raises his head and his eyebrows, and draws a deeper breath, as if he would yawn; he is half awake, and blowing upon the eyelids, or the repetition of the previous operation, or dusting the forehead by smart transverse wavings of the hand, or blowing upon it, causes the patient's countenance to become animated; the eyelids open, he looks about him, recognises you, and begins to speak. If any feeling of heaviness remains, any weight or pain of the forehead, another repetition of the same manipulations sets all right. And yet this patient would not have been awakened if a gun had been fired at his ear, or his arm had been cut off.

At the next sitting, or the next to that, the living statue begins to wake in its tranced life. The operator holds one hand over the opposite hand of his patient, and makes as if he would draw the patient's hand upwards, raising his own with short successive jerks, yet not too abrupt. Then the patient's hand begins to follow his; and, often having ascended some inches, stops in the air catochally. This fixed state is always relieved by transverse brushings with the hand, or by breathing in addition, on the rigid limb. And it is most curious to see the whole bodily frame, over which spasmodic rigidness may have crept, thus thawed joint by joint. Then the first effect shown commonly is this motion, the patient's hand following the operator's. At the same sitting he begins to hear, and there is intelligence in his countenance when the operator pronounces his name: perhaps his lips move, and he begins to answer pertinently, as in ordinary sleep-walking. But he hears the operator alone best, and him even in a whisper. *Your* voice, if you shout, he does not hear: unless you take the operator's hand, and then he hears *you* too. In general, however, now the proximity of others seems in some way to be sensible to him; and he appears uneasy when they crowd close upon him. It seems that the force of the relation between the operator and his patient naturally goes on increasing, as the powers of the sleep-walker are developed; but that this is not necessarily the case, and depends upon its being encouraged by much commerce between them, and the exclusion of others from joining in this trance-communion.

And now the patient—beginning to wake in trance, hearing and answering the questions of the operator, moving each limb, or rising even, as the operator's hand is raised to draw him into obedient following—enters into a new relation with his mesmeriser. He *adopts sympathetically every voluntary movement of the other.* When the latter rises from his chair, *he* rises; when he sits down, *he* sits down: if he bows, *he* bows; if he make a grimace, *he* makes the same. Yet his eyes are closed. He certainly does not see. His mind has interpenetrated to a small extent the nervous system of the operator; and is in relation with his voluntary nerves and the anterior half of his cranio-spinal chord. (These are the organs by which the impulse to voluntary motion is conveyed and originated.) Further into the other's being he has not yet got. So he does not *what the other thinks of, or wishes him to do:* but only what the other either does, or goes through the mental part of doing. So Victor sang the air which M. de Puységur only mentally hummed.

The next strange phenomenon marks that the mind of the entranced patient has interpenetrated the nervous system of the other *a step farther*, and is in relation besides with the posterior half of the cranio-spinal chord and its nerves. For now the entranced person, who has no feeling, or taste, or smell of his own, *feels, tastes, and smells every thing that is made to tell on the senses of the operator.* If mustard or sugar be put in his own mouth, he seems not to know that they are there; if mustard is placed on the tongue of the operator, the entranced person expresses great disgust, and tries as if to spit it out. The same with bodily pain. If you pluck a hair from the operator's head, the other complains of the pain you give *him.*

To state in the closest way what has happened: The phenomena of sympathetic motion and sympathetic sensation thus displayed are exactly such as might be expected to follow, if the mind or conscious principle of the entranced person were brought into relation with the cranio-spinal chord of the operator and its nerves, and with no farther portion of his nervous system. Later, it will be seen, the interpenetration can extend farther.

But, before this happens, a new phenomenon manifests itself, not of a sympathetic character. The operator contrives to wake the entranced person to the knowledge that he possesses new faculties. *He develops in him new organs of sensation,* or rather helps to hasten his recognition of their possession.

It is to be observed, however, that several who can be entranced cannot be brought as far as the present step. Others make a tantalizing half-advance towards reaching it *thus*, and then stop. They are asked,—"Do you see any thing?" After some days, at length they answer "Yes." "What?" "A light." "Where is the light?" Then they intimate its place to be either before them, or to one side, or above or behind them. And they describe the colour of the light, which is commonly yellowish. And each day it is pointed to in the same direction, and is seen equally whether the room be light or dark. Their eyes in the mean time are closed. And here with many the phenomenon stops. Others in this light now begin to discern objects held in the direction in which they see it. The range of this new visual organ, and the conditions under which it acts, are different in different instances. Sometimes the object must be close, sometimes it is best seen at a short distance; but seen it is. The following experiment, which is decisive, was made at my suggestion: A gentleman standing behind the entranced person held behind him a pack of cards, from which he drew several in succession, and, without seeing them himself, presented them to the new visual organ of the patient. In each case she named the card right. The degree of light suited to this new mode of vision is variable: sometimes bright daylight is best; sometimes they prefer a moderate light. Some distinguish figure and colour when the room is so dark that the bystanders can distinguish neither.

These observations, which are, however, only in conformity with similar evidence from many other quarters, I give on the authority of Mr. J. W. Williamson of Wickham, the gentleman to whom I have before alluded. The following accidental features, attending the manifestation of transposed senses, were further observed by Mr. Williamson :—

In most of the persons in whom Mr. Williamson has brought out transposed vision, the faculty has been located in a small surface of the scalp behind the left ear; and to see objects well, the patient has held them at the distance of five or six inches from and opposite to this spot. One young woman, who had been temporarily set aside under affliction for the loss of a relative, on the experiments being resumed, saw from all parts of the head, but confusedly, a broken and incomplete picture. On a subsequent day, she saw with the right side of her head. Afterwards the visual sense returned to its first place.

In one young person, the new sentient organ was on the top of her head, and to see objects she required them to be brought into contact with it. Once that she had a rheumatic cold and tenderness of the scalp, she said, when entranced, putting her hand to the crown of her head, that the cold had made her eyes sore.

One person saw objects best when placed behind her at the distance of seven or eight feet.

The governess in a neighbouring family was mesmerised for tic-doloureux. In seven sittings she was cured. At the second sitting, in her trance she exhibited displaced sensation. She could read with her finger-ends; her way was to hold the book open against her chest, the back of the book towards her, with one hand; then she passed a finger of the other hand slowly over each word, to read it.

The part-physical character of these phenomena is shown by an observation of Dr. Petetin's on the first of his cataleptic patients. At the time that the patient heard with the pit of her stomach, he found that if with the fingers of one, say the left hand, he touched the pit of her stomach, and whispered to the fingers of his right hand, the patient heard him; but if the left hand was removed to the smallest possible distance from the patient, the contact being interrupted, she no longer heard him. Then he made a chain of seven persons, holding each other's hands. The nearest to the patient was her sister, who touched the pit of her stomach; at the other end was Dr. Petetin, who whispered to his fingers, and was heard. A cane was then introduced as part of the circuit—the patient still heard; but if a stick of sealing-wax, or a glass rod, was substituted for it, or if one of the party wore silk gloves, the patient could no longer hear Dr. Petetin. Without close observation, what is physical in the phenomena which have thus engaged us is liable to be overlooked; and the bystander may class them as examples of lucidity, which they are not. Organic co-operation may be traced in them all. Thus, among Mr. Williamson's earlier experiments, he tried, sitting before the entranced person, (who had shown no lucidity,) by imaging strongly to himself a white horse, to force the image into her mind. When, being awakened, she had left the room, on her way she said to her fellow-servant, "What was it master said to me about a white horse? I am sure he said something." Mr. Williamson, on learning the maid's remark, supposed his mental operation had been successful. But the same experiment, when repeated, mostly failed. At last he found out why: It only succeeded when, in his mental urgency, he half made in his own throat the motions of the sounds that expressed the mental image. Then, and then only, the patient caught it. For her mind could not read his thoughts, but as yet had penetrated the inferior part of the nervous system only, the cranio-spinal cord; and, being there, had adopted sympathetically the voluntary impulses that were there performed; so she half-moved the muscles of her own vocal organs to express the idea, and from that—its imperfect expression—received it into her thoughts. No doubt the phenomenon of Victor's singing the words to M. de Puységur's mentally hummed air was the same with the above, and not one of mesmeric lucidity, the subject which we are now approaching.

But I pause;—and go no further.

For my object in these Letters, generally, has been to establish principles. And the phenomena of lucidity developed in artificial trance have been only the same as, and have not been as yet made more of than, the lucidity of catalepsy. No further principle has yet emerged from their study; and my special object in this Letter has been to persuade the opponents of mesmerism to do it justice; and I think I am most likely to attain my end by not attempting to prove too much.

So that nothing remains for me to do, but to observe the form in which these Letters were originally shaped, in recollection of the pleasant hours which the residence of your family at Boppard, during the winter of 1844–5, caused me, and to say finally,

DEAR ARCHY, Farewell.

LETTER XI.

SUPPLEMENTAL.—Abnormal neuro-psychical relation—Cautions necessary in receiving trance communications—Trance-visiting—Mesmerising at a distance, and by the will—Mesmeric diagnosis and treatment of disease—Prevision—Ultra-vital vision.

THE principal alterations made in "the Letters" for the present edition comprise an expansion of my account of "trances of spontaneous occurrence," and the introduction of greater precision into our elementary conceptions of the relations of the mind and nervous system.

Letters V., VI., VII., and VIII., establish that the most startling phenomena in popular superstitions, and the most wonderful performances by mesmerised persons, are but repetitions of events, the occurrence of which, as symptoms of, or as constituting, certain rare forms of nervous attacks, have been independently authenticated and put on record by physicians of credit. Letters II. and IX. exemplify the mode in which superstition has dressed up trance-phenomena; as letters III. and IV. display the contributions she has levied on sensorial illusions, the Od force, and normal exoneural psychical phenomena. Letter X. describes the method of inducing trances artificially, whereby they may be reproduced at pleasure, either in the interests of philosophical inquiry, or for important practical purposes.

I dedicate the present Letter to the reconsideration of the most knotty points already handled, and to the investigation of a few other questions, the solution of which is not less difficult.

I. *Hypothesis of an Abnormal Psychico-neural Relation as the essence of trance.*—I admit that it is a very clumsy expedient to assume that the mind can, as it were, get loose in the living body, and, while remaining there in a partially new alliance, exercise some of its faculties in unaccustomed organs—which organs lose, for the same time, their normal participation in consciousness; and farther, that the mind can, partially indeed, but so completely disengage itself from the living body, that its powers of apprehension may range with what we are accustomed to consider the properties of free spirit, unlimitedly as to space and time. I adopt the hypothesis upon compulsion—that is to say, because I see no other way of accounting for the most remarkable trance-phenomena. In due time, it is to be expected that a simple inductive expression of the facts will take the place of my hypothetical explanation. But not the less may the latter, crude as it is, prove of temporary use, by bringing together in a connected view many new and diversified phenomena, and planting the subject in a position favourable for scientific scrutiny.

Let me arrange, in their most persuasive order, the facts which seem to justify the hypothesis above enunciated.

1. In many cases of waking-trance, the patient does not see with his eyes, hear with his ears, nor taste with his tongue, and the sense of touch appears to have deserted the skin. At the same time, the patient sees, hears, and tastes things applied to the pit of the stomach, or sees and hears with the back of the head, or tips of the fingers.

2. In the first imperfect trance-waking from initiatory trance, the patient's apprehension of sensuous impressions

often appears to have entirely deserted his own body, and to be in relation with the sentient apparatus in his mesmeriser's frame—for, if you pull his hair, or put mustard in his mouth, he does not feel either; but he is actually alive to the sensations which these impressions excite, if the hair of the mesmeriser is pulled, or mustard placed on the mesmeriser's tongue. The sensations excited thus in the mesmeriser, and these alone, the entranced person realizes as his own sensations.

3. About the same time, the entranced person displays no will of his own, but his voluntary muscles execute the gestures which his mesmeriser is making, even when standing behind his back. His will takes its guidance from sympathy with the exerted will of the other.

4. Presently, if his trance-faculties continue to be developed, the entranced person enters into communication with the entire mind of his mesmeriser. His apprehension seems to penetrate the brain of the latter, and is capable of reading all his thoughts.

5. In the last three steps, the apprehension of the entranced person appears to have left his own being to the extent described, and to have entered into relation with the mind or nervous system of another person. Now, if the patient become still more lucid, his apprehension seems to range abroad through space, and to identify material objects, and penetrate the minds of other human beings, at indefinite distances.

6. At length the entranced person displays the power of revealing future events—a power which, as far as it relates to things separate from his own bodily organization, or that of others, seems to me to show that his apprehension is in relation with higher spiritual natures, or with the Fountain of Truth itself.

16

In the following pages I have given examples of those of the powers here attributed to very lucid clairvoyantes, which I have not previously instanced.

II. *Transposition of the Senses.*—No doubt these phenomena, irregular as they seem at present, follow a definite law, which has to be determined by future observations and experiments. Mr. Williamson found some of his clairvoyantes see with the back of the head, some with the side of the head—some best at seven inches, others at as many feet off. In the case which Mr. Bulteel reported to me, the lady read with her hand and fingers; even when he pressed a note against the back of her neck, she read it instantly: but in this case actual contact was necessary. In the case of a governess, artificially brought to the state of waking-trance by Mr. Williamson, the same faculty was observed. With one hand she used to hold open the book to be read, resting it against her chest, the pages being turned away from her: the contents of these she read fluently, touching the words with the forefinger of the other hand. In one very interesting case, which I witnessed here in the autumn of 1849, the young lady, clairvoyant through mesmerism, sitting in the corner of a sofa, something reclined, would have seen, had she peeped through a linear aperture between her seemingly closed eyelids, the lower half of things only. As it was, the reverse was the fact; and when we asked her what she saw, she told us the cornice and upper part of the room. Then, without saying any thing, I raised my cap upon my stick to within her declared range of trance-vision; she exclaimed, "Ah, Guilleaume Tell!" Her mother, whom she heard speak, but had not hitherto seen, in this trance, she recognised at once, when she stood up upon a chair. To read, in this trance, appeared a very painful effort to her; but she was certainly able to make out some words when she pressed a written paper against her forehead. It was evident that she could now visually discern things by some new faculty of apprehension localized there. To enable her to see things at a few feet distance, they had equally to be placed *opposite* to her forehead. In another case, in which the girl, when entranced, certainly saw with the knuckles of one hand, on smearing the back of that hand with ink, she could no longer see with it.

The above instances show how various are the features attending the transposition of one sense alone in waking trance; and they suggest a multitude of experiments. I remember, in 1838, on communicating facts of this kind to a clear-headed practical man, he raised this objection to their credibility: "If we can see without eyes, why has the Creator given us eyes!" The objection is specious enough, but it admits of an obvious answer. The state of trance is one of disease, transient and temporary; it is during its persistence only that this new power of apprehension is manifested. In our natural state, the mind is intended to operate and try experiences in subordination to matter, and through definite material organs, in which it is, in truth, imprisoned. Such is the law of our normal mortal being. Accordingly, when the trance is over, and the mind has returned to its normal relations with the body, all its trance-apprehensions are forgotten by it—they form no part of our moral life.

III. *Sources of Error in the communications of entranced persons.*—I put aside cases of deliberate deception; but when persons are really entranced, they are liable, in various ways, to be deceived themselves, and to deceive others, as to the value of their revealments. There is often, in waking trance, a great vivacity and disposition to be communicative from the first. Those, again, who have frequently been thrown into trance, and have become familiar with their new condition, are generally anxious to shine in it, and make a display. This disposition is further heightened when the entranced person expects to be rewarded for his performance.

1. When indulging their lively fancy, they are liable to have a sort of waking dream, during which they describe imaginary scenes with the precision and minuteness of reality, and represent them as actual, passing at some place they name.

2. They are liable to recall past impressions, and to deliver bits of old conclusions for intuitions.

3. They are liable to adopt the thoughts of others who may be near them, especially those of their mesmeriser, and to deliver them as trance-revelations.

4. In one instance which came to my knowledge, a young lady, previously unacquainted with mathematics or astronomy, would, when entranced, and sitting with her mother and sister, write fluently off pages of an astronomical treatise, calculations, diagrams, and all. She averred and believed in her entranced state—for, when awake, it was all a mystery to her—that this performance was the product of an intuition. Her manuscript was afterwards found to run word for word with an article in the *Encyclopædia Britannica*. That book, however, stood in the library, in a remote part of the house. She certainly had it not with her when she used to scribble its contents; nor did she remember ever having

looked into it, awake or asleep. She said—when entranced, and this had been found out—that she believed she read the book as it stood in the library.

5. With some imperfectly lucid patients, the exercise of their new faculties appears to be fatiguing, and to call for great exertion. So they are occasionally with difficulty led to answer at all; and then when inconsiderately pressed, they are tempted to say any thing, just to be left tranquil.

It is difficult to say how the preceding sources of error are to be effectually guarded against. Possibly, by rigid training from the first, the patient might be brought to distinguish false promptings from genuine intuitions. But even the latter vary in lucidity and certainty. This admission was made to a friend of mine by M. Alexis, the celebrated Parisian clairvoyante. The reader cannot fail to be interested by the following account, given by M. Alexis when entranced, of his own powers, and their mode of operation:—

"Pour voir des objets éloignés," observed M. Alexis, "mon âme ne se dégage pas de mon corps. C'est ma volonté qui dérige mon âme, mon esprit, sans sortir de cette chambre où je suis. Si mon âme sortit, je serais mort; c'est ma volonté. Ma volonté suffit pour anéantir pour quelque tems la matière. Ainsi quand cette volonté est en jeu, la boite matérielle de mon individu n'est plus. Les murs, l'espace, et même le tems, n'existent plus. Mais ce n'est qu'un rêve plus ou moins lucide. Quelquefois ma vue est meilleure qu'à d'autres. Ma vue n'est jamais la même. Une fois je suis disposé pour voir une sorte de choses, et une autre fois une autre sorte. En regardant votre chambre dans un quartier éloigné d'ici, je ne vois pas les rues ni les maisons intermédiaires. La seule chose (alors) qui est dans la pensée est la personne qui me parle. Je vois les objets d'une manière plus incomplète que par mes sens, moins sure. Il serait impossible de fair comprendre comment je vois. Plus il y a de l'attraction—plus j'éprouve de l'attraction aux objets que je veux voir, ou qui me touche—plus il y a de lumière; plus j'éprouve de répulsion, plus il y a de ténèbres."

IV. *Of the Different Qualities of Od in different individuals.*—Von Reichenbach observed the Od light to have different colours under different circumstances, and that, while Od-negative produces the sensation of a draft of cool air, Od positive produces a sense as of a draft of warm air. An easy way to verify the last phenomenon is to beg some one to hold the forefinger of the right hand pointed to your left palm, at a quarter of an inch distance, and afterwards his left forefinger to your right palm, when the two sensations, and their difference, are appreciable by the majority of persons.

Persons entranced by mesmeric procedures are often keenly alive to the above impressions. They see light emanating from the finger-tips of the mesmeriser, and feel an agreeable afflatus from his manipulations. Others who approach them affect them in different ways—some not disagreeably, while others excite a chilly, shivering feeling, and the patient begs they will keep off from him.

A gentleman narrated to me the following case. He had been for months in anxious attendance upon a brother who was in very delicate health, and exquisitely sensitive to mesmerism. My friend used himself to mesmerise his brother; but he found it necessary, in order to soothe and not excite him by the passes, to cover the patient with a folded blanket, so as to dull the agency of his Od-emanation. There was but another person, of several who had been tried, whose hand the brother could bear at all; this was a maid-servant, who herself was highly susceptible, and became entranced. She said that she perceived, when entranced, the suitableness of her influence, and that of the brother, to the patient; and she used the singular expression, that they were nearly of a colour. She said that the patient's Od-emanation was of a pink colour, and that the brother's was a brick colour—a flatter, deeper, red; and she endeavoured to find some one else with the same coloured Od to suit her master.

In some experiments made at Dr. Leighton's house in Gower Street, I remember it was distinctly proved that each of the experimenters produced different effects on the same person. The patient was one of the Okeys, of mesmeric celebrity. The party consisted of Dr. Elliotson, Mr. Wheatstone, Dr. Grant, Mr. Kiernan, and some others. Mr. Wheatstone tabulated the results. Each of us mesmerised a sovereign; and it was found that on each trial the trance-coma, which contact with the thus mesmerised gold induced, had a characteristic duration for each of us. Is it possible that each living person has his distinguishable measure of Od, either in intensity or quality?

V. *The Od-Force is the usual channel of establishing mesmeric relation.*—I take it for granted that the Od-force—the existence and some of the properties of which have been inductively ascertained by Von Reichenbach—is the same agent with that which Mesmer assumed to be the instrument in his operations. Then, in support of the above proposition, I cite two instances. Mr. Williamson, at my request, mesmerised and entranced the Rev. Mr. Fox at Weilbach, in the autumn of 1847. It was the second sitting, and Mr. Fox was beginning to pass from the initiatory stage of trance into trance half-waking. Mr. Williamson addressed him, and he returned an answer. Other parties in the room, including myself, then addressed Mr. Fox, and he seemed not to hear one of us. Then Mr. Williamson gave me his hand, and I again spoke to Mr. Fox; he then heard me, and spoke in answer. When, having left go Mr. Williamson's hand, I spoke again to Mr. Fox, he heard me not. On my renewing contact with Mr. Williamson, Mr. Fox heard me again. He heard me as long as I was brought into relation with him, and that relation was clearly due to the establishment of an Od-current between myself and Mr. Williamson, with whom Mr. Fox was already in trance-relation. Every one who has seen something of Mesmerism will recognise in the above story one of its commonest phenomena.

But a more conclusive instance still has been already mentioned in Letter X. M. Petetin made a chain of seven persons holding hands, the seventh holding the hand of a cataleptic patient, who at that time heard by her fingers only. When Dr. Petetin spoke to the fingers of the first, *i. e.* the most remote, person of the chain, the cataleptic person heard him as well as if he had spoken to her own fingers. Even when a stick was made to form part of the circuit, the cataleptic still heard Dr. Petetin's whisper, uttered at the other end of the chain. *Not so, however, if one of the parties forming the chain wore silk gloves.*

VI. *Trance-Identification of persons at a distance by means of material objects.*—A very lucid clairvoyante, her eyes being bandaged, recognises not the less, without preparation or effort, every acquaintance present in the room; describes their dress, the contents of their purses, or of letters in their pockets, and reads their innermost thoughts. An ordinary clairvoyante usually requires the contact of the party's hand with whom it is proposed to bring her into trance-relation; then only does she first know any thing about her new patient. It cannot be doubted that, in the latter case, it is the establishment of an Od-current between the two that enables the mind of the clairvoyante to penetrate the interior being of the visiter,—just as, in the humblest effects of common mesmerism, a relation is sensibly established between the party entranced and her mesmeriser, through the Od-current which he had previously directed upon her, in order to produce the trance. So far, all is theoretically clear enough.

But how is the establishment of the same relation between the clairvoyante and a party wholly unknown to her, and residing many miles off, to be explained, when the only visible medium of physical connexion employed has been a lock of hair or a letter written by the distant party, and placed in the hands of the clairvoyante? Let me begin by giving the explanation, and afterwards exemplify the phenomenon out of my own experience.

I conceive that the lock of hair, or the letter on which his hand has rested, is charged with the Od-fluid emanating from the distant person; and that the clairvoyante measures exactly the force and quality of this dose of Od, and, as it were, individualizes it. Then, using this clue, *distance being annihilated to the entranced mind,* it seeks for, or is drawn towards, whatever there is more of this same individual Od quality any where in space. When that is found, the party sought is identified, and brought into relation with the clairvoyante, who proceeds forthwith to tell all about him.

Now for an exemplification of this marvellous phenomenon. Being at Boppard, a letter of mine addressed to a friend in Paris was by him put into the hands of M. Alexis, who was asked to describe me. M. Alexis told at once my age and stature, my disposition, and my illness; how that I am entirely crippled, and at that time of the day, half-past eleven, A.M. was in bed. All this, to be sure, M. Alexis might have read in my friend's mind, without going farther. But, he added, this gentleman lives on the sea-coast. My friend denied the assertion; but M. Alexis continued very positive that he was right. Now, most oddly, the Rhine, on the banks of which I resided then, is at Boppard the boundary of Prussia; and I never cross it, or visit Nassau, but I am in the habit of sitting on the bank, listening to the breaking of the surge, which the passing steamers create, and which exactly resembles the murmur of the sea. This very mistake of M. Alexis helped to convince me that this performance of his was genuine. However, being stoutly contradicted by my friend, M. Alexis reconsidered the matter, and said, "No; he does not live on the sea-coast, but on the Rhine, twenty leagues from Frankfort." This answer was exact. But there was another point which M. Alexis hit with curious felicity. I should observe that this friend was one of a few months' date, who had no means of comparing what I am with what I was formerly. But it had happened that I had written, not to him, but to a friend resident in England, *about the same time*, that, ill as I was, my mind was singularly clear and active, and that I regarded the fact as a sign my end was at hand; that the mental brightness probably resembled the flaring-up of a rushlight before it goes out. Well, M. Alexis, adverting to my condition, observed that I was extremely weak, and had suffered much from irritation of the nerves;—facts true enough, but which certainly would not have led him to infer the existence of that clearness of mind which I had myself remarked. Nevertheless, strangely added M. Alexis, "Le morale n'en est pas atteint; au contraire, l'esprit est plus dégagé et plus vif qu'auparavant." I can therefore entertain no doubt, that at four hundred miles' distance, merely by handling a recent letter from me, M. Alexis had identified me as its writer, through the Od-fluid the letter conveyed; and had truly penetrated my physical and mental being so completely, that most that was important in my story lay distinctly revealed before him.

VII. *Mental Travelling by clairvoyantes.*—Let me begin with an instance. The following extract from the *Zoist* contains a very interesting narrative by Lord Ducie, which is exactly to the point:

"In the highest departments or phenomena of mesmerism, he for a long time was a disbeliever, and could not bring himself to believe in the power of reading with the eyes bandaged, or of mental travelling; at length, however, he was convinced of the truth of those powers, and that, too, in so curious and unexpected a way, that there could have been no possibility of deception. It happened that he had to call upon a surgeon on business, and when he was there the surgeon said to him, 'You have never seen my little clairvoyante.' He replied that he never had, and should like to see her very much. He was invited to call the next day, but upon his replying that he should be obliged to leave town that evening, he said, 'Well, you can come in at once. I am obliged to go out; but I will ring the bell for her, and put her to sleep, and you can ask her any questions you please.' He (Lord Ducie) accordingly went in. He had never been in the house in his life before, and the girl could have known nothing of him. The bell was rung; the clairvoyante appeared: the surgeon, without a word passing, put her to sleep, and then he put on his hat and left the room. He (Lord Ducie) had before seen something of mesmerism, and he sat by her, took her hand, and asked her if she felt able to travel. She replied, 'Yes;' and he asked her if she had ever been in Gloucestershire, to which she answered that she had not, but should very much like to go there, as she had not been in the country for six years: she was a girl of about seventeen years old. He told her that she should go with him, for he wanted her to see his farm. They travelled (mentally) by the railroad very comfortably together, and then (in his imagination) got into a fly and proceeded to his house. He asked her what she saw; and she replied, 'I see an iron gate and a curious old house.' He asked her, 'How do you get to it?' she replied, 'By this gravel-walk;' which was quite correct. He asked her how they went into it; and she replied, 'I see a porch—a curious old porch.' It was probably known to many, that his house, which was a curious old Elizabethan building, was entered by a porch, as she had described. He asked her what she saw on the porch, and she replied, truly, that it was covered with flowers. He then said, 'Now, we will turn in at our right hand; what do you see in that room?' She answered with great accuracy, 'I see a book case, and a picture on each side of it.' He told her to turn her back to the book case, and say what she saw on the other side; and she said, 'I see something shining, like that which soldiers wear.' She also described some old muskets and warlike implements which were hanging in the hall; and upon his asking her how they were fastened up, (meaning by what means they were secured,) she mistook his question, but replied, 'The muskets are fastened up in threes,' which was the case. He then asked of what substance the floors were built; and she said, 'Of black and white squares,' which was correct. He then took her to another apartment, and she very minutely described the ascent to it as being by four steps. He (Lord Ducie) told her to enter by the right door, and say what she saw there; she said, 'There is a painting on each side of the fire-place.' Upon his asking her if she saw any thing particular in the fire-place, she replied, 'Yes; it is carved up to the ceiling,' which was quite correct, for it was a curious old Elizabethan fireplace. There was at Totworth-court a singular old chestnut-tree; and he told her that he wished her to see a favourite tree, and asked her to accompany him. He tried to deceive her by saying, 'Let us walk close up to it;' but she replied, 'We cannot, for there are railings round it.' He said, 'Yes, wooden railings;' to which she answered, 'No, they are of iron,' which was the case. He asked, 'What tree is it?' and she replied that she had been so little in the country that she could not tell; but upon his asking her to describe the leaf, she said, 'It is a leaf as dark as the geranium-leaf, large, long, and jagged at the edges.' He (Lord Ducie) apprehended that no one could describe more accurately than that the leaf of the Spanish chestnut. He then told her he would take her to see his farm, and desired her to look over a gate into a field which he had in his mind, and tell him what she saw growing; she replied that the field was all over green, and asked if it was potatoes, adding that she did not know much about the country. It was not potatoes, but turnips. He then said, 'Now look over this gate to the right, and tell me what is growing there.' She at once replied, 'There is nothing growing there; it is a field of wheat, but it has been cut and carried.' This was correct; but knowing that, in a part of the field, grain had been sown at a different period, he asked her if she was sure that the whole of it had been cut. She replied, that she could not see the end of the field, as the land rose in the middle, which in truth it did. He then said to her, 'Now we are on the brow, can you tell me if it is cut?' She answered, 'No, it is still growing here.' He then said to her, 'Now, let us come to this gate—tell me where it leads to.' She replied, 'Into a lane.' She then went on and described every thing on his farm with the same surprising accuracy; and upon his subsequently inquiring, he found that she was only in error in one trifling matter, for which error any one who had ever travelled (mentally) with a clairvoyante could easily account, without conceiving any breach of the truth."

If the preceding example stood alone, or if, in parallel cases, no further phenomena manifested themselves, nothing more would be required to explain the facts than to suppose that the mental fellow-traveller reads all your thoughts, and adopts your own imagery and impressions. But there are not wanting cases in which the fellow-traveller has seen what was not in his companion's mind, and was at variance with his belief; while subsequent inquiry has proved that the clairvoyante's unexpected story was true. These more complicated cases prove that the clairvoyante *actually* pays a mental visit to the scene. But she can do more; she can pass on to other and remoter scenes and places, of which her fellow-traveller has no cognizance.

For example, a young person whom Mr. Williamson mesmerised became clairvoyant. In this state she paid me a mental visit at Boppard; and Mr. Williamson, who had been a resident there, was satisfied that she realized the scene. Afterwards I removed to Weilbach, where Mr. Williamson had never been. Then he proposed to the clairvoyante to visit me again. She reached, accordingly, in mental travelling, my former room in Boppard; and expressed surprise and annoyance at not finding me there, and at observing others in its occupation. Mr. Williamson proposed that she should set out, and try to find me. She said, "You must help me." Then Mr. Williamson said, "We must go up the river some way, till we come to a great town," (Mainz.) The clairvoyante said she had got there. "Then," said Mr. Williamson, "we must now go up another river, (the Maine,) which joins our river at this town, and try and find Dr. Mayo on its banks somewhere." Then the clairvoyante said, "Oh, there is a large house; let us go and see it; no, there are two large houses—one white, the other red." Upon this, Mr. Williamson proposed that she should go into one of the two houses, and look about; she quickly recognised my servant, went mentally into my room, found me, and described a particular or two, which were by no means likely to be guessed by her. When Mr. Williamson subsequently came to visit me at Weilbach, he was forcibly struck with the appearance of the two houses, which tallied with the account given beforehand by the mental traveller. I have not the smallest doubt she mentally realized my new abode. Then, how did she do all this?

The first question is, how does the clairvoyante realize scenes which are familiar to her fellow-traveller? I cannot help inclining to the belief that, in the *ordinary perception* of a place or person, the mind acts exoneurally; and that our apprehension (as I have ventured to conjecture in Letter V.) comes thus always into a direct relation with the place or person. There is a peculiar vividness in a first impression, which every one must have observed; there is no renewing that force of impression again. This fact helps my hypothesis. It will be remembered again, that in Zschokke's narrative of his seer-gift, he never penetrated the minds of his visiters unless at their very first visit. It is the same, even to a certain extent, with mesmeric inspection of the mind. My friend, who consulted M. Alexis for me, consulted him likewise for himself more than once. At the first visit, M. Alexis traced an aggravation of his illness, a year before, to distress occasioned by the death of two younger brothers at a short interval. On my friend's subsequent visits, M. Alexis marked no knowledge at all of the latter occurrence. Slightly as these facts are connected, they concurrently strengthen my notion of the occurrence of an exoneural act of the mind in common perception. I suspect, I repeat, that, in visiting new places, the mind establishes a direct relation with the scenes or persons. Then, in the simplest case of mental visiting, where the scene visited is familiar to the other party, I presume that the clairvoyante's mind, being in communion with the mind of the other, realizes scenes which the latter has previously exoneurally realized. Arriving thus at the scene itself, the clairvoyante observes for herself, and sees what may be new in it, and unknown to her fellow-traveller; and in the same way may pursue, as in the mental visit made to myself at Weilbach, suggested features of the locality, and be thus helped to beat about in space for new objects, and at length to recognise among them, and mentally identify, persons with whom she has already arrived at a mental mesmeric relation.

VIII. *Mesmerising at a Distance. Mesmerising by the Will.*—I have not heard of a case in which a person has been *for the first time* mesmerised with effect by one *out of the room.*

Generally the mesmeriser is very near to his patient at the first sitting, often actually holding his hand—at all events so near that the Od-emanation of his person might be expected to reach the patient. And the patient is often sensible of new sensations, which he is disposed to attribute to the physical agency of the operator on him. In Mr. Braid's cases, it seemed to me clear that the effects were mainly brought about, as in common mesmerism, by his personal influence.

Afterwards, when a patient has by use become highly sensitive to Od, and disposed to fall into trance, I have myself, by making passes *in the next room,* succeeded in producing the sleep. And I have seen, with open doors, mesmeric effects produced by passes at the distance of ninety feet.

But with persons rendered through use extremely susceptible of mesmeric impression, an effect may be produced by the habitual mesmeriser of the patient at almost unlimited distances. The following instance is given by Dr. Foissac in his valuable work on mesmerism, entitled

Rapports et Discussions sur le Magnétisme Animal, (Paris, 1838.) Dr. Foissac speaks, in the first person, of an experiment made by himself on a patient of the name of Paul Villagrand, whom he had been in the habit of mesmerising in the usual way at Paris, where both resided.

"In the course of the June ensuing," says Dr. Foissac, "Paul expressed the wish to pass some days in his native place, Magnac-Laval, Haute Vienne. I provided him with the means, and proposed to turn his journey to scientific account by attempting to entrance him at the distance of a hundred leagues. He was not to know my intention before the time came; but on the 2d of July, at half-past five P.M., his father was to give him a note from me, which ran thus—'I am magnetising you at this moment; I will awake you when you have had a quarter of an hour's sleep.' M. Villagrand made the success of the experiment the more decisive by not handing over my letter to his son, and so disregarding my instructions. Nevertheless, at ten minutes before six, Paul being in the midst of his family, experienced a sensation of heat, and considerable uneasiness. His shirt was wet through with perspiration; he wished to retire to his room; but they detained him. In a few minutes he was entranced. In this state he astonished the persons present, by reading with his eyes shut several lines of a book taken at hazard from the library, and by telling the hour upon a watch they held to him. He awoke in a quarter of an hour."

One naturally doubts whether the physical influence of the Od force can extend to this enormous distance; whether the agency ought not to be regarded as purely psychical; whether, in short, the will of the speaker may not have been the exclusive agent employed.

I think that there is a disposition, among experimenters in mesmerism, to attribute too much to the agency of the will. There was with me in the autumn of 1849 a young lady, who was extremely susceptible of mesmerism. A gentleman who came with the family had been in the habit of entrancing her daily, and at last she was so sensitive that a wave of his hand would fix her motionless. His presence even in the room affected her; and if he then tried to mesmerise her sister, she herself invariably became entranced. The operator was a person of remarkable mesmeric power. Then at my request, made unknown to her, he went to the end window of the room, and, looking out upon the Rhine, tried at the same time with the most forcible mental efforts to will her into sleep. The attempt failed entirely. Another day that he was in my room, about fifty feet from the room in which the young lady was sitting, he tried again by the will to entrance her. But it was all in vain. Therefore, if the will ever acts independently of Od influence, I am disposed to think that its action in producing trance must be infinitely feebler than the direct use of Od.

However, some are convinced of the positive agency of the will in mesmerising. The following statement by Mr. H. S. Thompson of Fairfield, made in a letter to Dr. Elliotson, published in the *Zoist*, admits the inferiority in force of the will to the material agency of Od, at the same time that it goes far to prove its efficiency.

"I have succeeded," says Mr. Thompson, "in arresting spasms, and taking away every species of pain, and in producing intense heat and perspiration, by the will only; and in many instances without the knowledge of the patients, who have been all unconscious of the power I have been exerting, until after the results have occurred.

At the same time, I have generally found that the passes in combination with the will, or attention, most readily produce the effects we desire; and that manipulations are much less fatiguing to the operator than the exertion of the will."

Of an extremely sensitive patient, who was suffering with rheumatic pains, Mr. H. S. Thompson observes, "A few passes put her to sleep, though she was moaning as in great pain, and scarcely seemed to notice what I was doing. After sleeping for a few minutes, her face became composed, and she showed no symptoms of pain; but as I could not get her to speak in her sleep, I awakened her. She looked very much surprised, and said that she felt very comfortable and free from pain. I told my friend that she was so sensitive that I thought that she might be put to sleep by the will in a few minutes. The bed-curtains were drawn, so that she could not see or know what was going on. I fixed my attention upon her, wishing her to go to sleep. When we looked at her two minutes afterwards, she was fast asleep. It was agreed that the following day, though I should be thirty miles off, the experiment should be tried again. A lady went at the time fixed on. I purposely postponed the time half-an-hour, thinking that the woman might have become acquainted with my intention, and go to sleep through the power of the imagination. The lady's account was, that she called upon the woman at the time agreed on, and at first thought that the experiment was going to fail, as she saw no symptoms of sleep; but that in half-an-hour afterwards the patient went into a deep sleep, which lasted some time. After this she went to sleep every day for a fortnight at the same time, though I did not will her to sleep. She says that she felt in a dreamy and happy state for some days after."

I might add many similar facts to the above interesting observations. The mass of evidence existing on the subject establishes beyond all doubt that patients have been thrown into trances by persons who have previously mesmerised them in the common way, at distances which seem to preclude the idea of any physical agent having been the medium of communication between the two parties. The operation seems to have been in those instances mental. Then how is such a result to be explained? —or by what expression can it be brought to tally with the principles I am endeavouring to substantiate? I shape the answer thus:—

The first step is ordinary mesmerising; in other words, the operator directs an Od-current upon the patient, the Od in whose system is thereby disturbed; and initiatory trance ensues as the consequence.

Secondly, The mind of the patient thus entranced enters into relation with, or is attracted towards, the mind or person of the mesmeriser. I remember witnessing a most decisive instance in which the operation of this attraction was singularly manifested. The place was Dr. Elliotson's waiting-room; the patient, a young man whom Mr. Simpson had entranced. Mr. Simpson then moved about the room, standing still at several points in it in succession. The young man seemed attracted towards Mr. Simpson, to whom he drew near each time he stopped; then he pressed against Mr. Simpson, jostling him out of his place, which he planted himself in—his countenance bearing an expression of huge delight at what he had achieved. But in half a minute he began to look anxious and uneasy; and again—his eyes being shut all the while —he set off in search of Mr. Simpson, and repeated the same scene. There exists, it would appear, an attraction between the (mind of the?) entranced person and (that of?) his mesmeriser, or (that of?) any other person with whom the entranced person has secondarily come into relation.

Then, thirdly, It may be presumed that, in phenomena which are purely mental, space and distance go for nothing. But if this supposition be admitted, it would be as easy for a mesmeriser to entrance by a mental effort a sensitive and habituated patient at a hundred miles off as at the end of the same room. The phenomenon thus viewed is wholly exoneural. The one mind is supposed to be actually sensitive to the influence of the other. Each of the two minds, though in different degrees, energizes, it may be imagined, beyond its bodily frame. And the mind of the patient feels the force of the mesmeriser's will acting upon it, and slips as it were at once, by the accustomed track, out of the normal into the abnormal psychico-neural relation.

Still I cannot get rid of a lurking notion that, in the phenomena last considered, the Od-force contributes an element of physical or physico-dynamic influence. For, putting for the moment aside the idea of mental action, what is to prevent two living bodies, that may be in Od-relation, or in exact Od-unison, from physically influencing one another at indefinite distances?

IX. *Trance-Diagnosis.*—From Boppard, where I was residing in the winter of 1845–6, I sent to an American gentleman residing in Paris a lock of hair, which Col. C—, an invalid then under my care, had cut from his own head, and wrapped in writing-paper from his own writing-desk. Col. C— was unknown even by name to this American gentleman, who had no clue whatever whereby to identify the proprietor of the hair. And all that he had to do and did was to place the paper, enclosing the lock of hair, in the hands of a noted Parisian somnambulist. She stated, in the opinion she gave on the case, that Col. C— had partial palsy of the hips and legs, and that for another complaint he was in the habit of using a surgical instrument. The patient laughed heartily at the idea of the distant somnambulist having so completely realized him.

The mesmeric discrimination of disease involves three degrees.

First, the clairvoyante placed in relation with the patient, either by taking his hand, or by handling a lock of his hair, or any thing impregnated with his Od, *feels all his feelings*, realizes his sensations, and describes what he sensibly labours under. Her account of the case thus obtained will be more or less happy, according to the extent of her previous knowledge respecting ordinary disease.

Secondly, the clairvoyante, if in a higher state of lucidness, actually sees and inspects the interior bodily construction of the patient, whose inward organs are, as it would seem, lit with Od-light, for her examination. Or she sees them by their Od-light, being in mesmeric relation with the internal frame of the patient.

Thirdly, the clairvoyante, if still more lucid, foresees what will be the progress of the malady; what further organic changes are threatened; what will be the patient's fate.

The first two points require no further comment. I reserve my comments upon the last for another head.

X. *Mesmeric Treatment.*—Let me first advert to the use of artificial trance as an anæsthetic agent in the service of surgery. There is no doubt that, when a patient can thus be deprived of ordinary sensibility, the resource is preferable to the employment of chloroform. Not only is it absolutely free from risk, but its direct effect is to soothe and tranquillize; whereas chloroform is but a powerful narcotic, the effects of which are obtained through a brief stage of violent physical excitement. Then, at each dressing—at any moment, in short, when advisable—mesmerism may be again resorted to, which chloroform cannot. The honour of having been the first to employ mesmerism systematically, as an anæsthetic agent, belongs to James Esdale, M. D., Presidency Surgeon at Calcutta. The reports of his success, in a vast body of cases, many of the most serious description, are given in the *Zoist.*

A second point is the employment of artificial trance as a universal sedative; as a means from which, in all cases purely nervous, the most admirable results may be expected and are realized; and from which, in disease in general, singular and beneficial effects have been obtained. This success was confidently to be anticipated, the instant that the real nature of mesmeric phenomena was appreciated.

A third point is the employment of mesmeric passes, without the intention or power to produce trance,—simply as a local means of tranquillizing the nervous sensibility of a diseased part, and allaying the morbid phenomena which depend upon local nervous irritation.

There is a fourth point under this head which will be regarded as more questionable, viz. the power attributed to clairvoyantes of prescribing treatment for themselves and others. Nevertheless, in their own cases, where the prescriptions have been limited to baths, and bleeding, and mesmerism itself, the boldness and precision of their practice, and its success, have been such as to excite our wonder, and almost to command our confidence. It does not, however, seem that the treatment prescribed by clairvoyantes to others is equally certain; and when they recommend drugs, it is clear that, adopting the fashion of the time and country in medicine, they are only prescribing by guess, like other doctors. But they sometimes guess very cleverly.

XI. *Phreno-Mesmerism.*—How great is my regret that I can no longer take an active part in physiological inquiry! How great is my regret that, in former years, when I worked at the physiology of the nervous system, I undervalued phrenology! Prejudiced against it by the writings of the late Dr. Gordon, by the authority of my early instructors, by the puerile mode in which craniology was generally advocated, by the superficial quality of the cerebral anatomy of Gall, I confined my attention to what I considered sounder objects of investigation. But now I have no doubt, not only that the metaphysical speculations of Gall were in the main just, but, likewise, that a great part of his craniological chart is accurately laid down. To connect phrenology with severe anatomical research, to endeavour to determine the organic conditions which interfere with the application of the science to practical purposes, would be a task worthy the efforts of the best physiological labourer. Then, if phrenology be true, and the organology in the main correct, what is more likely than that directing an Od current upon the cerebral seat of a mental faculty should bring it into activity? I have myself witnessed the repetition of this now common experiment, in a very unexceptionable instance; and the success was perfect. The organs of veneration, of combativeness, of alimentiveness, were successively excited; and in each case a brilliant piece of acting followed. I must confess, however, that I could not divest myself of the impression that, whatever pains we took to conceal our plans, the clairvoyant young lady really knew beforehand what was expected of her, and performed accordingly. I speak in reference to the single instance which I have myself witnessed. I cannot, however, refuse to credit the testimony of good observers—such as Dr. Elliotson—to facts which seem to establish the genuineness of phreno-mesmerism. In its double relation to phrenology and mesmerism, this inquiry well merits attention.

XII. *Rapport. Mesmeric Relation. Psychical Attraction.*—Without presuming to place absolute confidence in the preceding speculations, but, on the contrary, apologizing for their hypothetical character, on the plea that any theory is better than none, let me now recapitulatorily put in array the facts and principles to which the terms at the head of this section refer:—

1. I hold that the mind of a living person, in its most normal state, is always, to a certain extent, acting exoneurally, or beyond the limit of the bodily person; but, possibly, always in conjunction with some Od-operation.

2. I suppose that there must be laws of neuro-psychical attraction, or that there are definite circumstances which determine our exoneural apprehension to direct itself upon this or that object or person.

So, in common perception, the exoneural apprehension probably moves back along the lines of material impression, to reach the object perceived, which so attracts it.

So, in sudden liking or aversion at first sight—or,

more properly, on all occasions of meeting strangers—an exoneural mingling of reciprocal appreciation takes place; different persons being differently gifted with intuitive discernment, as others or the same with powers of pleasingly affecting most they meet.

So Zschokke's seer-gift would have been but the result of a greater exoneural mobility of his mind, whereby he was occasionally drawn to such mental affinity with a stranger, that he knew his whole life and circumstances.

So in panic fears, in all cases where impressions seem heightened by the sympathy of many, the power of psychical attraction we may presume to be increased by its concentration on one subject, and the participation of all in one thought. The Rev. Hare Townshend, in his interesting work on mesmerism, declares that he has more than once succeeded in the following fact of sympathetic mental influence. All the members of a party then present have conspired against an expected visiter; and when he came—carefully, at the same time, abstaining from alluding to some special subject agreed on—they have striven silently and mentally to drive it into his thoughts; and in a short time he has spoken of it.

3. For the most lucid persons in waking-trance (either of spontaneous occurrence, as in catelepsy, or when induced by mesmerism) the exoneural apprehension seems to extend to every object and person round, and to be drawn into complete intelligence of or with them. Such a patient is "en rapport," or in trance-mental relation with any or every thing around, in succession or simultaneously.

4. In persons slowly waking in the most measured course of things out of artificial initiatory trance into somnambulism, the mind is at first exoneurally attracted

to the mesmeriser alone. As a next step, the mesmeriser, by putting himself in Od-relation with a third person, can make him participator in the same attraction.

I do not here discuss Mr. Braid's views, which are more fully considered in a subsequent Letter. I have analyzed trance in its character of a spontaneous pathological phenomenon. I have examined its principal features as they present themselves when it is induced by mesmerism. But facts have been brought forward by Mr. Braid, which seem to establish that, in some highly susceptible persons, trance may be brought on at will in another way, by their own indirect efforts, apart from external influences:—as, for instance, by straining the eyes upwards, the attention being kept some time concentrated on the object or the effort. Certainly, doing this makes the head feel uncomfortable and giddy, and seems as if it would lead to some kind of fit if indefinitely prolonged.

XIII. *Trance-Prevision.*—Instances of trance-prevision are referrible to three different heads.

1. The simplest trance-prevision is that of epileptic patients (artificially entranced) who name, at the distance of weeks beforehand, the exact hour, nay, minute, at which the next fit will occur. The case of Cazot, (mentioned by Dr. Foissac,) who was in the habit of predicting the accession of his fits with unerring precision, terminated, however, in the following manner: Cazot had predicted, as usual, when he should be next attacked: before the time came round, however, he was thrown from a horse and killed. But no doubt can be entertained that, had he not met with this accident, the next fit would have occurred at the hour predicted. This is

the simplest and narrowest form of prevision: the clairvoyante can tell, in reference to himself, or to any one with whom he is placed in relation, what will be the course of his health. He can see forward what the progress of his living economy will be, *other things continuing the same.*

2. The next feat is greater. Dr. Teste, in his most interesting *Manuel de Magnétisme Animal,* gives the case of a lady, his patient, who, when entranced, foretold the day and hour when an accident, the nature of which she could not foresee, was to befall her, and from it a long series of illness was to take its rise. Dr. Teste and the lady's husband were staying with her when the fatal moment approached. Then she rose, and, making an excuse, left the room, followed by her husband; when, on opening a door, a great gray rat rushed out, and she sank down in a fit of terror, and the predicted illness ensued. In this most decisive case, the prevision extended to an extraneous and accidental circumstance, to which no calculation or intuition of her natural bodily changes could have led her.

3. But there are instances which reach yet farther. Dr. Foissac narrates the case of a Mdlle. Cœline, who, when entranced, predicted that she would be poisoned on a certain evening, at a given hour. What would be the vehicle of the poison she could not foresee, either at the time when she first uttered the prediction, or on an occasion or two afterwards, when, being again entranced, she recurred to the subject. However, shortly before the day she was to be poisoned, being questioned in trance as to the possibility of averting her fate, she said, "Throw me into the sleep a little before the time I have named, and then ask me whether I can discern where the

danger lies." This was done, and Mdlle. Cœline at once said that the poison was in a glass at her bed-side—they had substituted for quinine an excessive dose of morphine.

Thus it appears that persons in waking trance can, first, calculate what is naturally to follow in their own health, or in that of persons with whom they are in mesmeric relation; can, secondly, foretell the occurrence of fortuitous external events, without seeing how to prevent them; can, thirdly, when endowed with more lucidity, discern enough to enable them occasionally to counteract the natural course of external events. Fate thus becomes a contingency of certainties. There is a true series of consequences to be deduced from whatever partial premises the clairvoyante may happen to be acquainted with. When she has more data, she makes a wider calculation, certain as far as it goes. But other premises, influencing the ultimate result, may still have escaped her. So the utmost reach of genuine trance-prevision is but the announcement of a probability, which unforeseen events may counteract.

I will conclude this head by introducing M. Alexis's account of his own powers of mesmeric prevision, in which the reader will see that his experience has led him to view his conclusions as calculations upon certain positive elements; yet he admits the possibility of powers greater than his own: "On peut prévoir l'avenir," said M. Alexis; "mais lorsque cet avenir a des fondations positives. Mais annoncer un fait isolé, un accident, une catastrophe, non. Cependant quelquefois cela est arrivé aux individus, mais c'étaient des instruments de la Divinité: ces hommes sont rares. Etant à une maison de jeu, je saurais d'avance la couleur gagnante, surtout aux cartes,

Mais à la roulette cela me semble très difficile. Cela est de l'avenir. Les cartes, au contraire, sont dans les mains d'un homme quelques minutes. Cependant si l'on voulait appliquer la clairvoyance à une exploitation semblable, je suis materiellement et moralement certain que la vue ferait faute."

XIV. *Ultra-terrestrial Vision.*—If a clairvoyante can discern what is passing at the distance of one hundred leagues, why should not his perception extend to material objects beyond our sphere?

Mr. Williamson tried to conduct one of his clairvoyantes mentally to the moon; but, having got some way, she declared the moon was so intolerably bright, that the effort pained and distressed her, and accordingly Mr. Williamson relinquished the experiment, and happened not to renew it.

M. Alexis, when entranced, in answer to my inquiries, declared himself cognizant of the condition of the planets. He said that they were inhabited, with the exception of those which are either too near to, or too remote from the sun. He said that the inhabitants of the different planets are very diverse; that the earth is the best off, for that man has double the intelligence of the ruling animals in the other planets. It would be the height of credulity to regard this communication as more than a clever guess; yet a plausible guess it is, for if the other planets are composed of the same material elements with the earth, it is evident that the temperature of our planet must render these same materials more generally available for life and economic purposes on it than they would be in Mercury or Saturn.

XV. *Ultra-vital Vision.*—The following is M. Alexis's trance-revelation as to the state of the soul after death. I presume it is no more than an ingenious play of his fancy; but a young clergyman of some acumen, to whom I communicated it, was half disposed to give it more credit, and observed, with logical precision, that, viewing the statement as an intuition, it would show the necessity of the resurrection of the body.

"L'âme ne change jamais. Après la mort elle retourne à la Divinité. Dieu a voulu attacher l'âme au corps, qui est un prison où Dieu a voulu enfermer l'âme pendant qu'elle est sur la terre. L'âme ne perd jamais son individualité. Après la mort, nos souvenirs ne nous restent pas."

The last sentence is that to which my friend's remark principally referred.

XVI. *Nature of the Supreme Being.*—The following striking expressions were made use of by M. Alexis, when entranced, in answer to a string of questions which I had sent to him on this subject. He declared, at the same time, that he had never before been led to consider it in his mesmeric state. I presume, therefore, that in his ordinary waking state he is a Spinozist, and that, in place of an intuition, he simply delivered an oracular announcement of his preconceived notions:—

"Il n'y a pas de parole humaine qui peut donner une idée de la Divinité. Dieu c'est tout. Il n'a pas de personalité. Dieu est partout et nulle part. Dieu est le foyer qui allume la nature. Dieu est un foyer universel, dont les hommes ne sont que la vapeur la plus éloignée, la plus faible. Chaque homme est l'extremité d'un rayon de Lui-même. Il n'existe que Dieu."

LETTER XII.

THE ODOMETER OR DIVINING-RING.—How come upon by the author —His first experiments—The phenomena an objective proof of the reality of the Od-force.

"QUALIS ab incepto" shall be the motto of this twelfth letter, the materials of which were undreamt of by me, when some three months ago I remitted the new and corrected edition of "the Letters" to England. The occasion which led me to the knowledge of the facts I have to mention, and their bearing, tally curiously with what has gone before.

For it is again winter, with its long, solitary evenings, against the tedium of which I had to seek a resource; and I bethought me, this time, of occupying myself with looking into the higher mathematics. Accordingly I sent to Herr Caspari, professor of mathematics in the gymnasium at Boppard, to solicit him to give me the instruction and assistance which I needed. And he obligingly came, in the evening of the 31st of December, to sit by my side and converse with me. And I went over preliminarily my schoolboy recollections of the elements of mathematics, and was pleased at finding the remembered difficulties vanish before the explanations of my well-informed tutor. And I learned, to my vast delight, that the inability under which asymptotes labour to touch hyperbolas is a purely arbitrary one, like the legislative prohibition not to marry with one's deceased wife's sister; but that, unlike the latter, it can be evaded; inasmuch as an asymptote, by changing its name and forfeiting its properties, may at any time unite itself with the object to which it had before been infinitely near. Again, I found my boyish distrust and disbelief in sines and cosines replaced by an intelligent and well-satisfied acquaintance with them. And I even obtained a glimpse of the higher analysis itself, pointing with its unerring finger to the exact height, else unmeasurable, at which my candle should stand in the centre of my round table, to shed upon it its maximum of illumination.

A liberal hour being over, and my dolphin-like recreation ended, my new friend entered into desultory chat, and asked me, among other things, if I had not written something on the divining-rod. I replied to his question by giving him the copy I had of "the Letters;" and promised, as a New-Year's gift for the morrow, to present him with the implement itself. And I lent him Von Reichenbach's book on Od, with which he was unacquainted. Then he told me that there were two or three experiments, possibly akin to trials with the divining-rod, with which he had been familiar for years, and which he had shown to many without receiving an explanation of them. He said that as far as he knew they were original and his own; and that he would willingly show them to me. He wanted only for that purpose a piece of silver, a gold ring, and a bit of silk. These were easily found. And he attached the silk to the ring, which he then held suspended by the silk over a silver spoon, at a distance of half an inch.

Shortly the ring shaped its first vague movements into regular oscillations in a direction to and fro, or towards and from, Herr Caspari. I will call such oscillations *longitudinal.* It was evident to me, that this phenomenon must be akin to the motion of the divining-rod.

Then, at Herr Caspari's suggestion, I summoned the maid, who was directed to place her hand in Herr Caspari's disengaged hand. On her doing so, the oscillations of the ring became *transverse.* How pregnant was this fact! An Od-current had been established between the two experimenters; and the apparent influence of the two metals on each other had been modified.

Herr Caspari told me that, as far as he knew, these experiments would only succeed when made with silver and gold, and a bit of silk. But he said that he had still another experiment to show me, which he did the following day. He said he had a little pea-like bit of something, which he had been told was *schwefel-kies*, that exhibited another motion: when held suspended by silk over either of the fingers, it rotated one way; when held suspended over the thumb, it rotated in the contrary direction.

Herr Caspari left me, after agreeing to assist me in the further examination of these phenomena; and the New Year coming in found me in busy thought how to elicit, through variations of Herr Caspari's experiments, some important physical evidence as to the reality and agency of Von Reichenbach's Od-force.

In ten days we have succeeded in disentangling the confused results which attended our first experiments; and as I see no likelihood of extending them at present in any new direction, I present them to the reader now, as complete as I can at present render them. I have used the term "divining-ring," partly because I have a vague idea of having seen Herr Caspari's first facts adverted to in some publication under that name; partly because it is really thus far deserved:—If you place a piece of silver on a table, and lay over the table and it an unfolded silk pocket-handkerchief, you can discover where the silver lies by trying with the suspended ring each part of the surface. The ring will only oscillate when held over the silver. But now I have to substitute another name for the sake of precision.

A fragment of any thing, of any shape, suspended either by silk or cotton thread, the other end of which is wound round the first joint either of the fore-finger or of the thumb, I will call an *Odometer*. The length of the thread does not matter. It must be sufficient to allow the ring, or whatever it is, to reach to about half an inch from the table, against which you rest your arm or elbow to steady your hand. If there be nothing on the table, the ring or its equivalent soon becomes stationary. Then you test the powers of the odometer by placing upon the table under it what substances you please. These I would call *Od-subjects*.

To obtain uniform results with the Odometer, it is important to attach the sustaining thread always to the same finger of the same hand,—best to the fore-finger of the right hand. It is evident that this rule is not to prevent the experimenter, when he has succeeded in thus obtaining a series of consistent results, from trying what will come of substituting his other digits for that first employed.

I have armed the odometer with gold, silver, lead, zinc, iron, copper; with coal, bone, horn, dry wood, charcoal, cinder, glass, soap, wax, sealing-wax, shell-lac, sulphur, earthenware. As Od-subjects I have likewise tried most of the substances above enumerated. All do not go equally well, or perform exactly the same feats, with each odometer. For example, an odometer of dry wood remains stationary over gold; while it oscillates with great vivacity over glass. The respective habitudes of different odometers to different Od-subjects is one of the simplest points of investigation which the facts I am narrating suggest.

A gold ring with a plain stone in it was the first odometer which I employed, and it is one of the most largely available. And gold forms in general the most successful Od-subject. Sulphur likewise displays very lively motions in the odometer. But the material which I finally employed to verify the following phenomena was shell-lac, a portion a full inch long, broader towards the lower end, then cut to be lancet-shaped. The odometer moves more sluggishly with some than with others, and in the same hand on different days; and doubtless is capable of manifesting a greater variety of effects than I have yet elicited from it. I can only pledge myself to the certainty of my being always now able to obtain with the shell-lac odometer all the results mentioned in the XXVII. experiments which first follow. Over rock-crystal, however, the shell-lac odometer acts very feebly; but a glass odometer moves with brilliant vivacity. I would besides advise the reader to try a gold-ring odometer, in preference, for experiments X., XI., XII., XIII.

Then here are the results:—

I. Odometer (we will suppose armed with shell-lac) held over three sovereigns heaped loosely together to form the Od-subject; the odometer suspended from the right forefinger of a competent person of the male sex. *Result*—Longitudinal oscillations.

II. Let the experimenter, continuing experiment I., take with his unengaged hand the hand of a person of the opposite sex. *Result*—Transverse oscillations of the odometer.

III. Then, the experiment being continued, let a person of the sex of the experimenter take and hold the unengaged hand of the second party. *Result*—Longitudinal oscillations of the odometer.

IV. Repeat experiment I., and, the longitudinal oscillations being established, touch the forefinger which is engaged in the odometer with the fore-finger of your other hand. *Result*—The oscillations become transverse.

V. Repeat experiment I., and, the longitudinal oscillations being established, bring the thumb of the same hand into contact with the finger implicated in the odometer. *Result*—The oscillations become transverse.

VI. Then, continuing experiment V., let a person of the same sex take and hold your unengaged hand. *Result*—The oscillations become again longitudinal.

VII. Experiment I. being repeated, take and hold in your disengaged hand two or three sovereigns. *Result*—The oscillations become transverse.

VIII. Continuing experiment VII., let a person of the same sex take and hold your hand which holds the sovereigns. *Result* — The oscillations become longitudinal.

IX. If the odometer be attached to the thumb instead of to the forefinger, it oscillates longitudinally; but on approaching the thumb so as to touch the forefinger, the oscillations become of course transverse.

X. Repeat experiment I., but let the Od-subject be a double row of five sovereigns, each disposed longitudinally from you, and hold the odometer over the middle of the double row of sovereigns. *Result*—Longitudinal oscillations, but the excursions are inordinately long. Still, on touching the forefinger with the thumb, the oscillations become either transverse, or the odometer moves in an ellipse, of which the long axis corresponds with the axis of the double line of sovereigns.

XI. Dispose ten sovereigns longitudinally from you in two parallel rows, an inch and a half apart, and hold the odometer over the middle of the interval. *Result*—Longitudinal oscillations.

XII. Modify experiment XI. by holding the odometer not midway, but nearer one of the rows of sovereigns. *Result*—Oblique oscillations.

XIII. Dispose ten sovereigns heaped in a short longitudinal group, and hold the odometer over the table half an inch to one side of the middle of the heap. *Result*—Transverse oscillations.

From the latter experiments and their modifications, it became evident that the magnitude and shape of the Od-subject have each a direct influence on the result. A greater force of attraction evidently exists towards the greater mass.

XIV. Odometer held over the northward pole of a magnetic needle contained in a compass-box under glass. *Result*—Rotatory motion in the direction of the hands of a watch.

XV. Odometer held over the southward pole. *Result*—Rotatory motion in the direction contrary to the motion of the hands of a watch.

XVI. Repeat experiments XIV. and XV., with the difference of touching the forefinger implicated in the odometer with the thumb of the same hand. *Results*—The rotatory motions observed in the two experiments referred to become exactly reversed.

XVII. Hold the odometer over the centre of the needle. *Result*—Oscillations at right angles, or transverse, to the axis of the needle.

XVIII. Hold the odometer over, and half an inch to

one side of, the centre of the needle. *Result*—Oscillations parallel to the axis of the needle.

XIX. Repeat experiment XIV. Then, during its continuance, place a pile of three sovereigns on the compass-box, in front of the northward pole of the needle, and about an inch from it. *Result*—Direction of original rotatory motion reversed.

Then follow experiments with results exactly parallel to the preceding, having the greatest physiological interest.

XX. Hold the odometer over the tip of the forefinger of your disengaged hand. *Result*—Rotatory motion in the direction of the hands of a watch.

XXI. Hold the odometer over the thumb of your disengaged hand. *Result*—Rotatory motion against that of the hands of a watch.

XXII. Hold up the forefinger and thumb of the disengaged hand, their points being at two and a half inches apart. Hold the odometer in the centre of a line which would join the points of the finger and thumb. *Result*—Oscillations transverse to the line indicated.

XXIII. Modify the preceding experiment by holding the odometer half an inch to one side of, and over, the middle of the line indicated. *Result*—Oscillations parallel to the said line.

XXIV. Modify experiment XXIII. by approximating the ends of the forefinger and thumb of the disengaged hand, so that they touch. *Result*—The odometer no longer moves.

XXV. Forefinger and thumb of the disengaged hand held upwards and apart, sustaining a short file longwise between them. Odometer then held over the last joint of the finger. *Result*—Odometer stationary. Odometer then held over the last joint of the thumb. *Result*—Odometer stationary.

XXVI. Odometer held over the northward pole of the magnetic needle, and its consequent rotatory motion in the direction of that of the hands of a watch established. Then advance the finger or the thumb of the other hand towards the odometer. (The odometer should be held in these experiments half an inch above, and a little wide of, or before, the apex of the needle.) The finger, or the thumb, is then to be brought as near to the odometer as is consistent with not touching it in its rotation. *Result*—Direction of the rotation reversed. Then join the finger and thumb, and hold the two thus brought into contact in the same proximity to the odometer. *Result*—The rotation returns to the former direction; that is, to the direction of the motion of the hands of a watch.

XXVII. Odometer held over the radial (or thumb) edge of the wrist. *Result*—The same as when held over thumb. Odometer held over the little-finger edge of the wrist. *Result*—The same as when held over either of the fingers. This difference in result extends a third the length of the fore-arm, over the middle of which the odometer becomes stationary.

XXVIII. A portion of rock-crystal five inches long, about two wide and deep, placed on the table with its long axis transverse to the operator. Glass odometer held over the middle of the upper plain surface. *Result*—Oscillations parallel to the axis of the crystal. Position of the crystal shifted, so as to make its axis point *from* the operator. *Result*—Oscillations as before parallel to the axis of the crystal, but longitudinal to the operator. Then the thumb applied to the forefinger. *Result*—Transverse oscillations.

XXIX. Glass odometer held suspended over one apex of the crystal. *Result*—Rotatory motion in the direction of the hands of a watch. Odometer held over the opposite end. *Result*—Rotation in the direction contrary to that of the hands of a watch.

XXX. The last experiment repeated. The forefinger of the operator's unengaged hand brought near to the odometer in each of its two varieties. *Result*—The previous rotatory motion reversed. Then the point of the thumb brought into contact with the odometer finger. *Result*—The original rotatory motion re-established.

I will add in reference to the first and simplest experiments, that the interposition of several folds of silk between the Od-subject and the odometer renders the motions of the latter less brisk.

The development which I have thus given to the few, isolated, and long-hoarded experiments of Herr Caspari, was not so simple an affair as it may seem to be. For several days I was in doubt as to the genuineness of the results, so capricious and contradictory were they. It was only when I had discovered, first, the reversing effect of touching the odometer finger with the thumb of the same hand, and, secondly, that approaching the thumb towards the odometer finger, or even allowing the other fingers of the odometer hand to close upon the ball of the thumb, has the same effect with bringing the point of the thumb into contact with the odometer finger, that I succeeded in obtaining unvarying results. The interest of these experiments is unquestionably very considerable. They open a new vein of research, and establish a new bond of connexion between physical and physiological science, which cannot fail to promote the advancement of both. They contribute a mass of objective and physical evidence to give support and substantiality to the subjective results of Von Reichenbach's experiments. They tend to prove the existence of some universal force, such as that to which he has given theoretical form and consistence under the designation of Od. And such a universal force, what other can we deem it to be than the long-vilipended influence of Mesmer, rendered bright and transparent and palatable by passing through the filter of science?

LETTER XIII.

THE SOLUTION.—Examination of the genuineness of the phenomena —Od-motions produced by bodies in their most inert state—Analysis of the forces which originate them—Od-motions connected with electrical, magnetic, chemical, crystalline, and vital influences —Their analysis.

THE present letter might be entitled "An account of some motions recently discovered, to the manifestation of which an influence proceeding from the living human body is necessary." The contrivance by which these motions are elicited I have called an Odometer, from the conviction that the force which sets it in movement is no other than the Od-force of Von Reichenbach. For the same reason I have called the objects with which it is tested Od-subjects, and the motions themselves Od-motions.

The odometer is a pendulum, formed of a ring, or other small body attached to a thread, the other end of which is wound round a finger or the thumb. The odometer employed in the following experiments was a light gold ring, having a greater mass of metal on the unattached side, and suspended to the last joint of the right fore-finger, the suspending medium being either silk, or fine cotton, or the hair of a horse. The experiments were made by myself. In order to avoid the confusion resulting from a multiplicity of details, I shall state the results obtained through testing a limited number only of Od-subjects, so selected as to represent the leading divisions of the provinces of nature, and of dynamics. With some of the principal the reader will be already acquainted through Letter XII., the contents of which will have prepared him for, and probably suggested to him, the following question, as a desirable subject of preliminary consideration.

I. Are the motions referred to worth examining at all? Are they more than the simple results of impulses conveyed to the pendulum by movements of the hand or wrist, or some general sway of the experimenter's person, unintentionally going with the expectation or conception of this or that motion of the ring? Such a solution of the phenomena is not wanting in probability. It is metaphysically and physically certain, that when we maintain one and the same bodily posture or gesture, as in standing, sitting, or holding out the hand, whatever be the seeming continuousness and unity of the effort, the posture or gesture is really maintained only by a series of rapidly succeeding efforts. What is more likely than that, in such a continual renewing of voluntary actions, our fancy, or the sympathy between our will and our thoughts, should give a bias to the results, even when we most try to neutralize its influence? The fact which I propose first to mention is in complete agreement with this view. I can at will cause the odometer to move exactly as I please. Although I hold my hand as steadily as possible by leaning the arm against a table, and endeavour to keep my person absolutely still, yet I have only to form a vivid conception of a new path for the odometer, and a motion in the so-imagined direction is almost immediately substituted for that which was before going on. In like manner, I have only to conceive the cessation of motion, and the odometer gradually stops. I must farther admit that my first trials of the odometer were made under the full expectation that the results which ensued would follow. And I cannot say that it is impossible, that when other and new motions emerged, they were not often either realizations of a previous guess, or repetitions on the same principle of what occurred at first as an accident.

On the other hand, I am not unprepared with an array of facts which seem to me capable not only of neutralizing the force of the preceding argument, but of making it appear, most likely, that some other influence than that of the experimenter's mind is often in operation in bringing about these results; an influence sufficiently curious, as I think, to justify me in continuing this investigation and the present letter. I beg the reader's candid construction of the following statements.

If, when trying the odometer, I have caused it, by conceiving a different motion, to change its path and move in a *wrong* direction, I now endeavour to divert my mind from considering its motion at all, the odometer invariably resumes its previous *right* movement. It is, indeed, difficult to observe a strict mental neutrality in this instance. For the odometer moves imperfectly and uncertainly, unless I frequently look at its performance. Or, as I interpret the fact, unless I keep my attention fixed to a certain extent on what I am doing, my hand loses its steadiness, and communicates all sorts of distracting impulses to the pendulum. And the uncertainty hence arising admits, it appears to me, of being obviated by the comparison of numerous careful repetitions of the experiments.

Many of the motions which I at first thought were

genuine Od-results, I afterwards found out I had been mistaken in. And the correction of these errors was mostly due to frequent and careful repetitions of the experiments, unattended by an expectation of finding the results reversed or otherwise modified, and instituted simply to secure their genuineness and certainty.

Then there was one result which at one time I confidently anticipated; but it never came up. I had found the ring make gyrations in the direction of those of the hands of a watch, when held over the small end of a living unincubated egg. Opposite gyrations were obtained over the big end. I thought this might have to do with the sex of the embryo. And I tried, accordingly, a dozen eggs, expecting that in some the direction of the gyrations at the two ends would be reversed. But this event never occurred, much as I laid myself out for it. If my fancy could have decided the matter in spite of my care to prevent its interference, I am clear that for a time, at least, I should have obtained in these experiments upon the egg a double set of results. I was much delighted two months later at coming upon the explanation of the question, why gyration like that of the hands of a watch is manifested at the little end of the egg. I had known from nearly the first that this direction of the rotatory Od-motion is manifested when the pendulum is swung over the right side of the human body. Then I fell upon an old physiological reminiscence, (and found a drawing of the fact in my outlines of Physiology,) that the embryo chick lies in the egg transversely upon its face, with its right side towards the little end.

Then there were two other results, which were directly at variance with my anticipations, but which never failed to present themselves. I made a voltaic arrangement by means of two plates, one of zinc, the other of copper, fixed in contact in a solution of salt in water. Now, when held opposite the middle of the zinc disc, the odometer always rotated like the hands of a watch; while over the copper disc the phenomenon was reversed. These results are constant. But I have had the satisfaction of lately discovering that, if I present the ring to any part of the *circumference* of the two discs, its motion is the opposite, and in accordance with theory.

One of the tests on which I have much relied in determining whether the motions I obtained were genuine Od-motions, consisted in producing their reversal by altering the Od-relations of my hand or of my person. What gives particular value to this test is, that the versed or complimentary motion is subject to different laws. One set of secondary oscillations changes into oscillations in a plane at right angles to the plane of the primary oscillations. In another series the motion continues in the same plane; but the excursions, which were before longest in one direction, are now longest in the opposite, as if a repellent current had been substituted for an attracting one. The Od-oscillations, it may be observed, are always dependent upon the action of a constant rectilinear force counteracted by the gravitation of the pendulum. The means I usually employ to reverse the primary od-motions is, bringing the end of the right thumb into contact with the odometer-finger, where the thread is wound round it. But the experimenter cannot be too careful not to bring the thumb even near to the odometer finger, or to allow his other fingers to close upon the ball of the thumb, for the phenomena are thus again liable to be reversed.

The other means of reversing the results of the experiments are:—

a. To substitute a hair of a mare for the suspending media above-named.

b. To hold a sovereign in the left hand.

c. To apply the fore-finger of the left hand to the odometer finger.

d. To have either hand of a person of the same sex laid on your right hand or right ear.

e. To have either hand of a person of the opposite sex laid upon your left hand or left ear.

The various substances employed as Od-subjects admit of being divided into two great classes; one consisting of unorganized or organized bodies in which a minimum of internal activity is present; the other, of bodies of both classes, in which the more energetic properties of matter are at work.

I. Let me first notice the results obtained with the first class of bodies. These, again, are reducible to two forms. The Od-subject may either be of a regular figure and equal thickness throughout—as a piece of money, for instance; or it may be of an irregular figure, with an unequal mass of matter at one part—as, for instance, when it consists of an aggregate of several pieces of money variously arranged. I shall first treat of the first and simpler case.

It does not matter how you face in making these experiments. The influence of your person makes the various meridians of the Od-subject. The movements which we have first to examine are the results of holding the odometer over the middle of various uniform discs, such as I have supposed. They consist of two series of oscillations—one directed longitudinally to and from the experimenter; the other transversal, or in a plane at right angles to the plane of the first series of oscillations. Then it is highly convenient to have terms denoting the four cardinal points at which these oscillations cut the edge of the circular disc. These points may be termed *distal, proximal, dextral, sinistral.* It will likewise be found convenient to have terms to denote the direction of the motions manifested. The terms *distad, proximad, dextrad, sinistrad,* will serve our purpose. These terms refer to the person of the experimenter. Two other terms are still wanting; sometimes rotatory motion supervenes, which may be either in the direction of the motion of the hands of a watch, or the reverse. I call the first of these two motions *clock-rotation,* the second *versed-rotation.*

The present class of Od-subjects present the following remarkable differences among themselves:—

Over one class, including gold, zinc, and polished glass, a circular mass of bi-carbonate of soda, the odometer primarily oscillates *longitudinally.*

With the other class, which includes pearl, ground glass, copper, a circular mass of tartaric acid, the odometer held over the centre primarily oscillates *transversely.*

Over polished glass, an odometer of resin oscillates transversely; over ground glass longitudinally.

Each of these movements is replaced by the other, when the thumb is brought into contact with the odometer-finger. (See figs. 1 and 2, in which the continuous line represents the primary motion; the dotted line, the secondary or complementary or reversed motion.)

II. Analysis of the forces, or currents conducing to, or implicated in the movements of the odometer just described.

It has been said that the above movements manifest

themselves when the odometer is held over the centre of the Od-subject. Let us now examine the consequences of holding the odometer extra-marginally to, or beyond the edge of, the Od-subject.

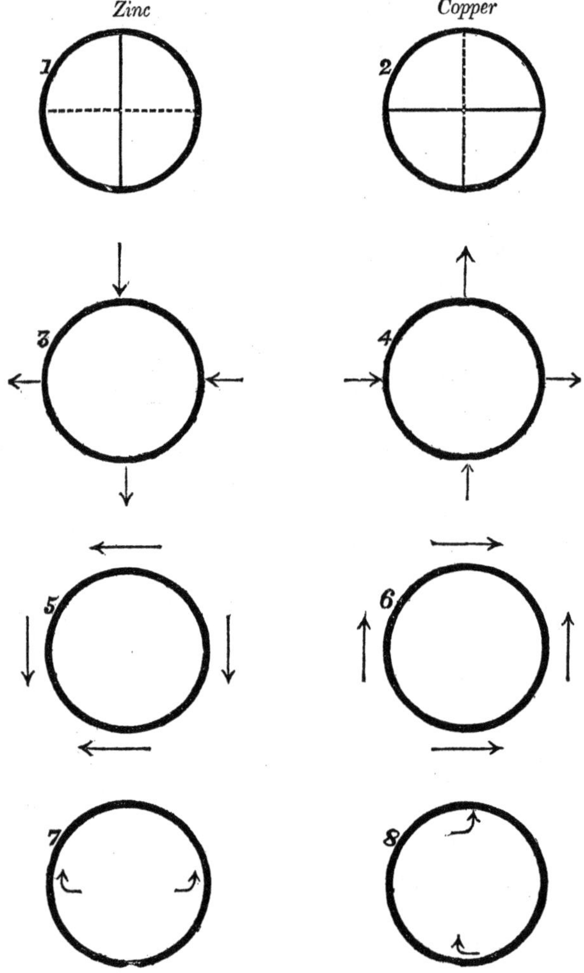

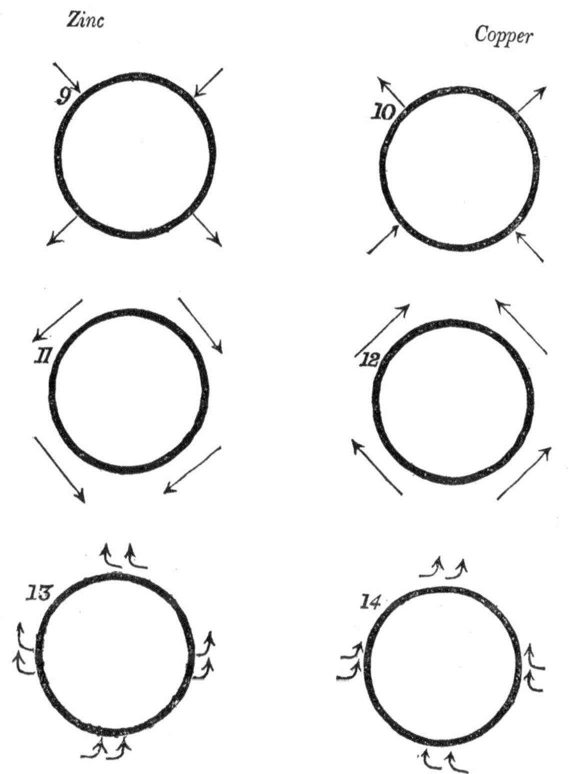

a. Let the odometer be held a quarter of an inch away from, and over each cardinal point of a sovereign, or zinc circular disc, in succession. *Result*—Held near the distal point, its motion is *proximad.* Held near the proximal point, its motion is *proximad.* Held near the dextral point, its motion is *sinistrad.* Held near the sinistral point, its motion is *sinistrad.* (See fig. 3.)

But the first two impulses thus attained correspond with the direction of the primary oscillations of the odometer, the last two with its complementary oscillations;

and if the odometer be held now over different points in succession of the two diametral lines, suspended, of course, by the finger alone over the first series of points, and by the finger touched by the thumb over the second, it will be found that the primary oscillations originated over every point of the longitudinal diameter of the zinc disc are proximad; and that those obtainable over any part of the transverse diameter of the zinc disc are sinistrad.

Then the forces or currents are made manifest by which the two sets of oscillations are produced; and the marvel of the prompt substitution of one for the other is at an end; for it is evident that these two forces, whether produced or only revealed by the presence of the odometer, co-exist; and that the changed Od-relations of the experimenter to the odometer, (effected by disjoining the thumb from, or joining it to, the forefinger,) simply act by giving temporary predominance to one of the two co-existent currents.

If these experiments be made at the edge of the copper disc, they elicit opposite but parallel results. (See fig. 4.) They evince the existence of two currents, one *dextrad*, the other *sinistrad*, from which the same conclusions may be deduced.

It is important to notice, that in all this class of the experiments, the distad and dextrad currents are manifested in combination; and in like manner the proximad and sinistrad.

This combination is further exemplified in the next experiment, which I shall describe.

b. Excite the above extra-marginal motions of the odometer held near the two plates in succession; and then apply the thumb to the finger in each experiment. *Result*—Tangential motions are manifested parallel to the diametral motions before displayed. (See figs. 5 and 6.)

We cannot, however, suppose these extra-marginal tangential motions to be the lateral limits of the four great currents, inasmuch as they are obtained by the versed process to that which obtains the central motion; and the question arises, what then are the limits of the central currents?

c. Hold the odometer over the zinc disc at its centre; of course, longitudinal oscillations determined by the proximad current manifest themselves. Then shift its place on the transverse diameter more and more to the left. *First Result*—For something more than a quarter of the whole diameter, the motion continues longitudinal, proving that the central current has a breadth at least something exceeding half the diameter. Same result on the other side of the centre. *Second Result*—When the odometer nears the sinistral cardinal point of the zinc disc, its longitudinal proximad motion is replaced by the motion I have called clock-rotation. When it is held near the dextral cardinal point, versed rotation manifests itself.

This second result establishes that the longitudinal proximad current extends laterally to the edges of the disc; but that, when near to them, the force of the co-existing transverse current asserts itself, driving the odometer (on the left) off in a sinistro-proximad diagonal, which ends in the establishment of clock-rotation; on the right driving the central current off, in a dextro-proximad diagonal, resulting in versed rotation. (See fig. 7.)

Parallel and opposite results are obtained by the odometer when these experiments are repeated with the copper disc; and necessarily the clock-rotation appears near the proximad margin of the disc, the versed rotation near the distal edge.

Therefore it is evident that the great longitudinal and transverse currents extend over the whole disc, but not beyond it. Experiment *a*, section II., and figs. 3 and 4, show that, immediately beyond the cardinal points, single forces are in operation.

Other interesting results follow from trying with the odometer the extra-marginal spaces between the cardinal points.

d. First let the central points between each pair of cardinal points be tried with the zinc disc. *Result*—(see fig. 9,)—a dextro-proximad current is manifested between the sinistral and distal points, and between the proximal and dextral points; a sinistro-proximad current is manifested between the dextral and distal, and between the proximal and sinistral points—giving the impression that there exist two diagonal forces, comparable to the longitudinal and transverse forces.

Fig. 10 gives the corresponding, but opposite, results obtained upon the copper disc.

It is, however, doubtful whether these currents traverse the whole disc. For if the experiment is made of following each upon the disc, their influence disappears at less than a quarter of the diameter, where the odometer is found to obey on the zinc disc the proximad current, on the copper disc the dextrad current. Or, probably, these currents are the simple expression of the action of two equal forces moving the body operated on by them (at right angles to each other) in the diagonal. These effects thus form a remarkable contrast with the results given in figs. 7 and 8, wherein rotatory movements are manifested; and they seem to show that an essential element in these rotatory movements is, that one of the two currents acting on the odometer must, in the latter case, be of superior force to the other.

e. Repeat the last experiments versed, or with the thumb applied to the forefinger. *Results*—(see figs. 11 and 12)—Tangential forces are developed, the directions of which are opposite, as obtained over the zinc and over the copper discs.

f. Repeat the extra-marginal trials of the odometer in all the halves of the inter-cardinal spaces, both with the zinc and with the copper discs. (See figs. 13 and 14.) *Result*—A complicated series of rotatory movements, eight for each disc; four in each case showing clock-rotation—four versed rotation—but opposite in the corresponding spaces of the two discs. On applying the thumb to the odometer finger, the rotations become exactly inverted; so that, in that case, fig. 14 represents what is now manifested in the zinc disc, fig. 13 what is now manifested in the copper disc.

III. Motions of the odometer obtained over the same class of substances, when of irregular figure and unequal thickness.

a. Let the odometer be held over the middle of a line of four sovereigns disposed either longitudinally, transversely, or obliquely. *Result*—Long oscillations over the axis of the line of sovereigns. But the oscillations are not of equal length. At one end of the line they extend to the edge of the fourth sovereign. At the other, they pass an inch beyond it.

b. Repeat the experiment, touching the odometer-finger with the right thumb. *Result*—Axial oscillations as before, and unequal as before, but in the contrary direction.

c. Dispose four sovereigns in a line; then place two others upon any one of the four, and hold the odometer over the table at three inches to one side of the middle of the line. *Result*—The odometer swings in each instance towards that sovereign on which the two additional are placed—but unequally. We will suppose that it has swung with sufficient strength to reach the disc of the loaded sovereign,—the oscillation in the contrary direction is but two inches in length.

d. Repeat the experiment, with the thumb applied. *Results*—Oscillations ensue of the same length, and they are again unequal, but in the contrary direction. Now they do not reach the pile of sovereigns by an inch, but they pass three inches in the opposite direction.

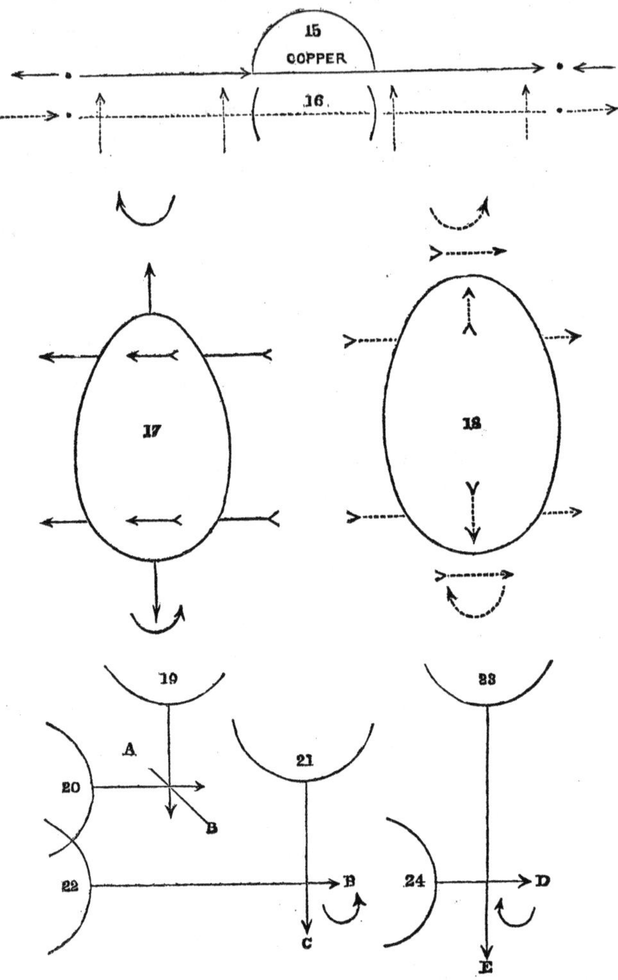
15
COPPER
16.
17
18
19
20
A
B
21
22
B
C
23
24
D
E

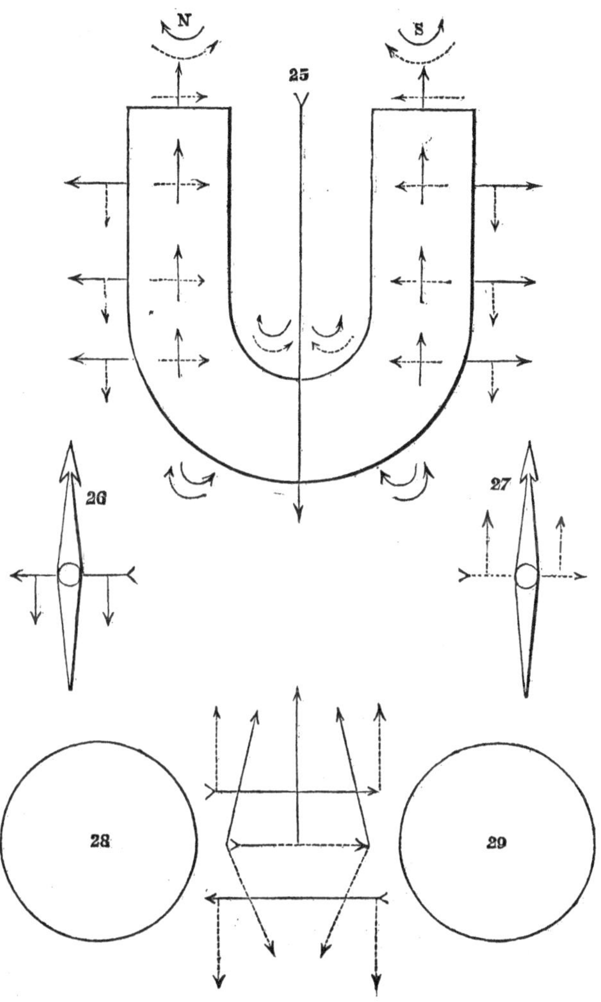
N
S
25
26
27
28
29

Thus a force is brought into view having this new quality: when the Od-relations of the experimenter are versed, a change ensues, not into motion in a plane transverse to the former one, but the direction of the new motion is simply the opposite of the first, or the odometer appears to be attracted or repelled towards the Od-subject alternately.

e. Try the same experiment with a single sovereign, or with the zinc disc. *Result*—The odometer held at four inches distance is attracted and repelled just as in the preceding instance.

Then an irregular form of the Od-subject, or its unequal mass at different parts, have nothing to do with this new motion; and it is evident that the relation of the latter to the former class of oscillatory motions will be easily determinable.

f. Lay the proper disc before you (see fig. 15,) and hold the odometer over the production in each direction of its transversal line beyond the limits of the disc. *Results*—When held near the right edge of the disc, as before mentioned, a dextrad motion is developed; that is to say, the odometer moves off from the dextral cardinal point of the disc, oscillatively. This movement, or those oscillations outward, are fainter and fainter, as the odometer is held over points more and more remote from the disc. At length, at the distance of an inch and a half, the odometer becomes absolutely stationary. When moved, however, still farther off, motion begins again, which is very lively at four to five inches distance from the disc, its direction being sensibly toward the disc. Moved farther off, still the same motion continues, and is detectable ten to twelve inches off the Od-subject.

When the same experiments are made on the left edge of the Od-subject, phenomena just the reverse are manifested for the same distance. The extra-marginal dextrad motion is transverse for an inch and a half. Then there occurs a point of quiescence; on the other side of which the odometer swings in free and long sinistrad or repelled oscillations.

g. Repeat these experiments (fig. 16,) with the thumb applied. *Result*—On the left side the near extra-marginal dextrad motion is replaced by a tangential proximad motion; and the centrifugal oscillations beyond the point of quiescence are replaced by centripetal oscillations. On the right side again, the near dextrad extra-marginal oscillations are replaced by a proximad tangential current: while beyond the point of quiescence, the remote centripetal oscillations are reversed into centrifugal ones.

Effects parallel to these are attained at each of the cardinal and intercardinal points of the whole circumference, upon the zinc or copper disc, but as usual always reversed.

Opposite to the eight intervening spaces, the character of the remote motion is changed. *There* it is a rotatory motion in a direction the reverse of the rotatory motion shown in figs. 15 and 16.

Thus, there exists all round the disc, at a distance of about an inch and a half, a circle of complete repose. Within this the proper, or near, extra-marginal movements of the odometer are manifested: without it, the motions of the second and remote force last described.

But to return to the facts mentioned at the beginning of this section.

The movements of the odometer over a line of sovereigns, or from a distance towards its centre of gravity, are evidently the consequences of this remote force coming into operation; the long and forcible oscillations caused by which toward or from a remote point override the smaller near extra-marginal, and the super-discal forces of the Od-subject.

IV. I have next to deal with the effects obtained by trying the odometer with mineral bodies, in which electric, chemical, or magnetic forces are energizing, or that force on which crystalline structure depends, and with organized bodies in possession of life.

In this section, I propose to describe the simple resultants, analogous to the two diametral movements, obtained when the odometer is held over a sovereign. It will be remembered that, of these two, one only manifested itself at a time; and that their meridians were determined by the person of the experimenter. One movement was either in the direction of the mesial plane of his person, or in one parallel to it—namely, the longitudinal oscillations; the other was in a plane at right angles to the first.

The corresponding movements of the odometer with the class of bodies now to be considered are rotatory; and two, at least, are always simultaneously manifested—one a clock rotation, the other a versed rotation. These opposite rotations are likewise always manifested on opposite sides or opposite ends of the Od-subject, indicating the development of polarity. Finally, the force of this polarity is such as to render the influence of the person of the experimenter nugatory as to the direction of the forces. Accordingly, if a horse-shoe magnet is laid in any position in reference to the experimenter, clock-rotation is always obtained by holding the odometer half an inch above, and beyond its northward pole; and versed rotation is invariably obtained in like manner at its southward pole. The effect of touching the odometer-finger with the thumb is exactly to reverse the two rotations.

I will now describe the individual instances in which

these rotations are manifested; or the parts of each Od-subject over which the odometer rotates in opposite directions.

CLOCK-ROTATION.	VERSED-ROTATION.
a. A stick of sealing-wax excited by friction with flannel or silk. A glass tube excited by rubbing it with fur.	A glass tube similarly excited.
b. The zinc disc of an arrangement of two zinc and copper discs moistened with salt and water, the odometer being held opposite to the middle of the zinc disc; for if it be held beyond the disc, half an inch from and on the exact level of the zinc disc, versed-rotation is manifested round the whole circumference.	The copper disc of the same, the odometer being held over against the surface of the copper disc; for again, if it be held to the edge of the copper disc, the opposite result follows, and the rotation is clock-rotation.
c. A mixture of half a drachm of bicarbonate of soda and five grains of tartaric acid, when effervescing upon a plate after the addition of water.	A mixture of half a drachm of tartaric acid and five grains of bicarbonate of soda.
d. The northward pole of a horse-shoe magnet, or of a magnetic needle freely suspended.	The southward pole of the same.
e. One pole of a large crystal, *which*, is to be found out by this experiment.	The opposite pole.
f. The root of a garden weed freshly taken from the ground.	The leaves of the same.
g. The stalk end of an orange, and of an apple, and of an orange pip.	The opposite points of the same.
h. The small end of an egg.	The large end of the same.
i. The tips of the fingers on either hand, and of the toes of either foot.	The top of the thumb and great toe.
k. Right side of the head of a sparrow.	Left side.

The last holds likewise with the greater part of the

human body; but the results of trying the odometer with the human frame are so complicated, that I shall reserve their consideration for a separate section.

V. The mechanical solution of these phenomena is simple enough. The odometer must be under the influence of two constant and unequal rectilinear forces, operating at right angles to each other on the gold ring, the effects of which are modified by the centripetal force of its gravitation. All that is required is, to determine by observation the place, direction, and limits of the two forces.

It will render the description which follows easier, to suppose that the pole of the Od-subject which causes clock-rotation be turned directly from the experimenter; for example, that an egg be placed longways to the experimenter with its small end from him, or a bar magnet with its northward pole from him. In the case of a horse-shoe magnet, both poles are then turned from you. So, too, in the case of the hand, the fingers and thumbs are both to be turned away.

a. Odometer held immediately before, and a quarter of an inch from, the small end of an egg. *Result*—Distad motion, or motion in the direction of the long axis of the egg, from the egg.

b. Odometer similarly held to the great end. *Result*—Proximad motion of the odometer—that is, again, motion directly from the axis of the egg.

c. Hold the odometer near either side of the egg, one-fifth of the distance from either end. *Results*—Transverse sinistrad oscillations. The same current may be detected above the egg on the same parallels.

The effects described are given in fig. 17. Then here are, at either end of the egg, two rectilinear currents acting at right angles to each other. Fig. 18 represents the complementary motions to the above, which are obtained by touching the odometer finger with the thumb. A parallel combination of rectilinear motions is produced, but in another way.

The next three figures exemplify the composition of forces necessary to produce the rotatory motion of the odometer.

Figs. 19 and 20 are intended to represent the large ends of two eggs, so placed that the axial currents of the two shall cross at right angles, at a point equidistant, let us say at half an inch exactly, from the end of each egg. If the ring be suspended exactly at the point of meeting of the two forces, it will be driven off in the diagonal, and continue simply to oscillate in the line A B. But if either of the eggs is moved back to double its former distance from the point of intersection of the two forces, the forces will be rendered unequal, and new results will ensue. The two experiments by which the results of this arrangement may be tried are represented in figs. 21, 22, and figs. 23, 24. The longer current is necessarily thereby the weaker of the two in each combination. Accordingly, rotatory motion supervenes in each case instead of diagonal oscillation; and the direction of the rotation is from the stronger towards the weaker current.

Figure 25 represents the various motions which may be elicited by holding the odometer at the sides or over different parts of a horse-shoe magnet. The continued lines in all the diagrams represent the primary motions, the dotted lines their complementary motions.

Figures 26 and 27 represent, in the same way, the primary and secondary oscillations obtainable over the centre of, or parallel to the needle.

Figures 28 and 29 represent the motions displayed by

the odometer, when it is held above various points in the interval between two sovereigns, placed upon the table an inch and a half asunder. Compound effects follow, produced by the joint influence of the two bodies.

VI. I will finally describe the phenomena elicited by the odometer from the living human frame, including those which are dependent on difference of sex.

Parties to experiments with the odometer may be in the position either of Od-subjects, or of reversers of its effects in the hands of others, or they may be themselves components of the odometer.

I can discover absolutely no difference in the results obtained by the odometer on men and women, when treated as Od-subjects. The following results appear to me equally obtainable with persons of both sexes.

With the exception of the arms below the elbows, the wrists and hands, and of the legs below the knees, the ankles and feet, the two sides of the person display the polar differences already noticed. If the odometer be held over the right side of the head, (either front or back,) over the right side of the face, over the right shoulder or elbow, or right knee, it exhibits clock-rotation. Held over the same parts on the left side, it exhibits versed-rotation. On touching the odometer-finger with the thumb, these effects are of course reversed.

If the odometer be held over the middle and outside of either arm, or over the middle and back of either fore-arm or hand, it oscillates longitudinally and towards the hand or foot. On reapplying the thumb, these longitudinal oscillations are replaced by transverse oscillations, having a direction *outwards—i. e.*, away from the mesial plane of the frame.

The phenomena last described show that the primary

idea of a transverse polarity for the whole frame is still verifiable, even in the extreme parts of either limb. But below the elbows and knees a second polarity is superinduced upon the former. Below the elbows and knees, one side of each limb repeats the phenomena of the right side of the body, the other those of the left. The odometer held over the tips of the fingers of either hand exhibits clock-rotation, over the thumb of either hand versed-rotation; and with these, as I have mentioned, all the other effects that can be elicited out of the two limbs of a horse-shoe magnet. The same rotatory movements may likewise be obtained by holding the odometer near the two edges of the hand, wrist, forearm. The latter singularity, which contrasts with the simpler effects on the upper arm, must result from the combination of the two polarities—the systemic and the submembral one.

The odometer, held over the back of the neck or throat, oscillates transversely. When versed, longitudinally.

It appears to me now that women generally are incapable of eliciting the movements of the odometer when held by themselves, without touching a second party.

I have already, in the introductory part of this letter, given a summary of all the modes I am acquainted with of reversing the motions of the odometer.

Perhaps I have presumed too much in heading this letter with the title of "The Solution." But what is the solution of physical phenomena but the displaying of the forces which compel their sequence? As an inquiry progresses, a few general expressions take the place of the first imperfect and complicated explanation. But the first step made was still a solution; and the highest solution ever yet obtained has probably still to be merged in some expression yet more general. So the attraction of gravitation is probably connected with, or balanced by, a corresponding repulsive force, coming into operation at some enormous distance from the centre of each planetary sphere, and the two may eventually prove to form one law.

But I had hoped that I was not presuming in asserting that the present inquiry has immediate practical applications, such as seldom fall to the lot of so young an investigation. The odometer may prove a useful test of the presence and qualities of electric, chemical, and magnetic actions; it will probably help to determine the electro-chemical qualities of bodies; and in large or small crystalline masses—in the diamond, for instance—will serve to show the axes and distinguish the opposite poles. In reference to biology, it will probably furnish the long-wanted criterion between death and apparent death; for I observe that, with an egg long kept, but still alive, though no longer likely to be very palatable, the odometer freely moves in the way described in the fourth section. But it treats the freshest egg, when boiled, as if it were a lump of zinc.

Nevertheless I am not without certain misgivings. I suspect that the divining-ring will be found to manifest genuine Od-motions in the hands of as small a number as succeed with the divining-rod. And I fear that overhasty confidence in results only seemingly sound, may lead many astray into a wide field of self-deception.

POSTSCRIPT.

An accident has given me the opportunity of making further additions to this little volume, of which I proceed to avail myself; and, first, by communicating my latest experiments with the divining-ring, July 24.

I. I have stated that, if a fresh egg be placed upon the table, with the small end directed *from* me—or a crystal, with one definite pole so turned from me—or a bar-magnet, with its northward pole so disposed—and I then suspend the divining-ring half an inch above either of the three so averted ends, and half an inch further off from me, the ring exhibits clock-rotation in each instance. Held in a parallel manner over the opposite ends—that is, half an inch from, and half an inch higher than, the same—the ring exhibits versed-rotation. If the three Od-subjects be moved round, so that their hitherto distal ends point to the right, or if they be further turned, so as to bring the previously distal ends now to point directly *towards* me, the ring continues to exhibit exactly the same motions as in the first instance.

If, these objects being removed, I lay a horse-shoe magnet on the table before me, with its poles turned directly *from* me, the northward limb being on my left hand, the southward limb-pole on my right, and experiments parallel to those just described are made, the results remain the same. If, near one side of the horse-shoe magnet, I lay my left hand on the table, the palm downwards, the thumb held wide of the fingers, the ring, if suspended half an inch from and above either of the finger-points, displays clock-rotation; suspended similarly before and above the point of the thumb, versed-rotation. Or the fingers of the left hand, so disposed, may be compared, in reference to Od, to the northward pole of a horse-shoe magnet, while the thumb corresponds with its southward pole.

If, removing my left hand, I turn the horse-shoe magnet, without altering the side on which it rests, half round, so that the poles point directly *towards* me, the northward pole being now, of course, on my right, the southward pole on my left, the ring held as before over either of the two poles, displays the same results. If I now move the magnet still nearer to me, so that its two poles are an inch beyond the edge of the table, I can obtain results which furnish a more precise explanation of the two rotatory movements already described, than I had before arrived at.

If I now suspend the ring, with its lowest part on a level with the magnet, and half an inch from its northward pole—that is, half an inch nearer me—it begins to oscillate longitudinally, with a bias towards me, as if it were repelled from the pole of the magnet. If I then suspend the ring an inch vertically above the first point of suspension, it begins to oscillate transversely, with a bias towards the right, or as if impelled by a dextrad current. If I then lower the ring half an inch, the first effect observed is, that it oscillates obliquely, being evidently impelled at once to the right and towards me—that is, in the diagonal of the two forces, of each of which I had before obtained the separate influence. In this third variation of the experiments, I have brought the ring to the limit of the two currents, where both tell upon it. This oblique oscillation soon, however, undergoes a change: it changes into clock-rotation, showing that the transverse or dextrad current is stronger than the longitudinal or proximad current.

If parallel experiments be made at levels below that of the pole of the magnet, corresponding but opposite results ensue. If the whole series be repeated upon the south pole of the magnet, opposite but perfectly corresponding results are again obtained: and similar results may be obtained with the two poles of an egg.

II. The mode in which I have latterly educed the rotatory movements depending upon galvanism, has been this. I have laid two discs, one of zinc, the other of copper, one on the other, having previously moistened their surfaces with salt and water. Then, as I mentioned, the ring held over the middle of the zinc disc (that being uppermost) exhibits clock-rotation. Held over the middle of the copper disc, when that is laid uppermost, versed-rotation. I mentioned, too, that if held beyond, but near the circumference of the same discs, the direction of the motion of the ring is reversed.

The discs which I employ are circular, an inch and a half in diameter, and about as thick as a sovereign. Upon these I do not fail to obtain, when dried and used singly, the first series of phenomena described in the preceding letter. But it occurred to me to try what would be the result of suspending the ring over the two together, and alternately laid uppermost, when they had been well cleaned and dried. This is evidently a still simpler voltaic arrangement than when the salt and water is additionally used. The result was in the highest degree interesting. When I suspend the ring half an inch above the centre of the copper disc, (that being laid uppermost,) the first motion observed is transverse; but after a few oscillations it becomes oblique—dextrad and proximad combined, in the diagonal between the primary influences of the zinc and of the copper. This change does not last long; the transverse force again carries it, in this instance, and clock-rotation is permanently established. When the zinc is uppermost, the corresponding opposite phenomena manifest themselves; and in either case a reversed movement occurs, if the ring is held extra-marginally to the discs.

III. I may say that I have now obtained positive evidence that these motions of the odometer do not depend upon my own will, or the sympathy of my will with existing conceptions in my mind; for they succeed nearly equally well when the discs are covered with half a sheet of writing-paper. In nine cases out of ten, when I thus manage to be in perfect ignorance which disc, or what combination of the two, is submitted to the odometer, the right results manifest themselves, and the cause of the occasional failures is generally obvious. Let me add upon this topic, that one day, the weather being cold and wet, and myself suffering severely with rheumatism, the odometer would not move at all in my hand. On another day, late in the evening it was, when I happened to be much fatigued and exhausted, the ring moved, indeed, but every motion was exactly reversed; thus my left hand I found now obtained exactly the results which, on other occasions, I got with the right.

IV. But by what cause, then—through what mechanism, so to speak, are the movements of the odometer immediately produced? Early in the inquiry I made this experiment. Instead of winding the free end of the silk round my finger, I wound it round a cedar-pencil, and laid the latter upon the backs of two books, which were made to stand on their edges, four inches apart, with the Od-subject on the table between them, the ring being suspended half an inch above it. The ring, of course, remained stationary. Then I took hold of the pencil with my finger and thumb, at the point where the silk was wound round it; my finger and thumb rested on the silk; but no motion of the odometer ensued. Hence it follows, that the odometer is, after all, always set in motion *by the play of my own muscles.* I venture then to suppose that my sentient nerves, unknown to me, detect on these occasions certain relations of matter—let me call them currents of force—which determine in me *reflexly* certain sympathetic motions of the very lightest, and even of an unconscious character. This idea, which I am sure affords the just solution of the matter, is highly consistent with some observations which I have before recounted. It explains how the primary delicate impression should yield to the coarser influence of a strong conception in the mind, that this or that other motion of the ring is about to follow, or even to that of a vivid and, so to say, abstract conception of another motion. It explains what I have several times verified, that on certain days a person standing behind me with his hand on my ear, or on my shoulder, can, by an effort of his will (mine not resisting,) make the odometer which I am holding move whichever way he happens strongly to image to himself, without communicating the same to me. It explains to me on what the difference consists between those who can set the divining-ring in motion, without a conscious effort, and those who cannot. The former, it will be found, are persons of so great nervous mobility, that any such motions, if their occurrence be forcibly anticipated by them, will certainly be realized by their sympathetic frames. Among this class should be sought, and would still remain to be detected by experiment, those whose *impressionability by Od should prove commensurate with their nervous mobility.* Finally, I cannot doubt that the view which I have thus arrived at respecting the mechanism of the motions of the odometer, is equally applicable to the explanation of those of the divining-rod. I see that, through its means, many before anomalous facts, with the narrative of which I have not bored the reader, which emerged in my former trials of the divining rod, made by the hands of others, lose their obscurity and contradictoriness, and leave the whole subject in the condition of an intelligible and luminous conception.

N. B.—It is a pity that of the inquirers who now amuse themselves with investigating these subjects, very few realize in their minds the idea of Von Reichenbach, that Od, though often exhibiting the same relations with electricity and magnetism, is yet an utterly different principle.

LETTER XIV.

Hypnotism. Trance-Umbra.—Mr. Braid's discovery—Trance-faculties manifested in the waking state—Self-induced waking clairvoyance—Conclusion.

It is an advantage attending a long and patient analysis of, and cautious theorizing upon, a new subject of inquiry, that when fresh facts and principles emerge in it, instead of disturbing such solid work as I have supposed, they but enrich and strengthen it, and find, as it were, prepared for them appropriate niches. Something of this satisfaction I experience, when I have to render tardy justice to Mr. Braid's discovery, and to give an account of the wonders realized by Dr. Darling, Mr. Lewis, and others.

Or, I have observed, that trance, considered in reference to its production, has a twofold character. It presents itself either as a spontaneous seizure brought on unexpectedly by a continuance of mental or physical excitement or exhaustion; or as intentionally induced through the systematic direction by some second person, more or less cognisant what definite effects he can produce, of certain moral and physical influences upon the party intended to be wrought on. Mr. Braid has added a third causal difference to the theory of trance. He has shown that trance can be induced by the subject of it himself voluntarily, by the use of certain means, which call into operation a special principle. The effects which he obtained by these means, but which he perhaps studied too much to separate from the effects of mesmerism—these and their principle he denominated *Hypnotism*.

Again, I have shown that all the forms of trance may be, and require to be, arranged under five types—viz., death-trance, trance-coma, initial trance, half-waking trance, full-waking trance. I mentioned, besides, that in the manifestation of Zschokke's seer-gift, and in the accounts which we receive of the performances called second-sight, the extended exoneural perception was introduced by a brief period, in which the performer was *in a degree* absorbed and lost, yet did not pass on into a second and separate phase of consciousness. He was still always himself, and observed and remembered as parts of his natural order of recollections the impressions which then occurred to him. This same state must be that which I have seen described as one peculiarly suited to the exhibition of phreno-mesmerism. Mr. Braid appears likewise often to have brought it on in his curative applications of hypnotism. But now it has new importance and distinctness conferred upon it, as being the state in which the wonderful phenomena of "mental suggestion" are best displayed, and in which conscious clairvoyance is manifested. As this state does not amount to complete trance, but as it is a fore-shadowing of it, as it were, I venture to propose for it the name of trance-umbra.

I. *Hypnotism.*—Mr. Braid discovered that if certain sensitive persons fix their sight steadily upon a small bright object, held near and above the forehead, or their sight becoming fatigued, and the eyelids fall, if they keep their attention strained as if they were still observing the same object, both in the upward direction of the eye and in their thought, they lose themselves and go off into a state which, in its full development, is, in fact, initial trance, bordering often on trance-coma. The party thus fixed sometimes exhibited many of the humbler performances of ordinarily mesmerised persons. But Mr. Braid shall speak for himself; I quote from his *Neurhypnology*, published in London in 1843. "I requested," narrates Mr. Braid, "a young gentleman present to sit down, and maintain a fixed stare at the top of a wine-bottle, placed so much above him as to produce a considerable strain on the eyes and eyelids, to enable him to maintain a steady view of the object. In three minutes his eyelids closed, a gush of tears ran down his cheeks, his head drooped, his face was slightly convulsed, he gave a groan, and instantly fell into profound sleep—the respiration becoming slow, deep, and sibilant, the right hand and arm being agitated by slight convulsive movements," (p. 17.) Again, (p. 18,) "I called up," continues Mr. Braid, "one of my men-servants, who knew nothing of mesmerism, and gave him such directions as were calculated to impress his mind with the idea, that his fixed attention was merely for the purpose of watching a chemical experiment in the preparation of some medicine; and being familiar with such he could feel no alarm. In two minutes and a half his eyelids closed slowly with a vibrating motion, his chin fell on his breast, he gave a deep sigh, and instantly was in a deep sleep, breathing loudly. In about one minute after his profound sleep, I roused him, and pretended to chide him for being so careless, said he ought to be ashamed of himself for not being able to attend to my instructions for three minutes without falling asleep, and ordered him down stairs. In a short time I recalled this young man and desired him to sit down once more, but to be careful not to fall asleep again, as on the former occasion. He sat down with this intention; but at the expiration of two minutes and a half, his eyelids closed, and exactly the same phenomena as in the former experiment ensued." Mr. Braid adds, "I again tried the experiment of causing the first person spoken of to gaze on a different object to that used in the first experiment, but still, as I anticipated, the phenomena were the same. I also tried on him M. Lafontaine's mode of mesmerising with the thumbs and eyes, and likewise by gazing on my eyes without contact; and still the effects were the same."

It is indeed perfectly obvious that Mr. Braid succeeded in producing a heavy form of initial trance in these cases. Nor is it easy to get rid of the impression that the effect was not partly at least owing to his personal Od influence. But, remembering what I witnessed of his performances, and construing candidly all his statements, I am disposed to believe that his method, adopted by the patient when in a room alone, upon himself, would throw susceptible persons into trance. Mr. Braid appears to me to have the double merit, first of having discovered the means of self-mesmerising—of so disturbing by very simple and harmless means the nervous system, that trance would appear without the influence of a second party to aid its supervention—and secondly, of having, at an early period, when prejudice ran very high in England against these practices, availed himself of this disguised mesmerism to do much good in the treatment of disease. Mr. Braid does not appear to have fallen on any instances of clairvoyance, but he narrates many observations relating to phreno-mesmerism.

II. *Trance-Umbra.*—This is the best title I can hit on to designate the peculiar condition, the study of which promises to exceed in interest that of any of the phases of perfect trance; inasmuch as in this state the same extraordinary powers are manifested as in trance, without the condition of an abstracted state of consciousness, which rendered the possession of those powers useless, at least, directly, to the person who manifested them. It is true that this law could be broken; the mesmeriser can desire an entranced clairvoyante to remember, when she awakes, any particular event or communication made by her. But for this exceptional power a special injunction or permit is necessary. In trance-umbra, on the contrary, the subject is throughout *himself*. When exhibiting the wildest phenomena he is conscious of what he is doing, and preserves afterwards as accurate a recollection of it as any of the spectators.

Then, how is trance-umbra induced? How is it known that the shadow of trance has enveloped the patient, and that, though quite himself to all appearance, he is in a state to manifest the highest trance-faculties?

The way to induce trance-umbra, is to administer a little dose of mesmerism. One operator, like Dr. Darling, (I quote from Dr. Gregory's most instructive and interesting *Letters on Animal Magnetism,*) directs his patient to sit still with his eyes fixed, and his attention concentrated on a coin held in his hand, or on a double-convex bit of zinc with a central portion of copper so held. This is, in truth, a gentle dose of hypnotism. The patient looks in quiet repose at a small object held in his hand or his lap, instead of fatiguing his sensations by straining the eye-balls upwards. Suppose a group of a dozen persons sitting thus in a half-darkened, still room, preserving a studied quietude, and concentrating their attention on one point of easy vision; in from fifteen to twenty minutes one or more is found to be in the state of trance-umbra. Mr. Lewis (I quote again the same authority) employs a different process. He eyes his patients intently as they sit in a row before him, still and composed, with a concentrated will, and its full outward expression by him, to influence their psychical condition. In five minutes it often happens that the state of trance-umbra supervenes.

In the mean time, what has marked its arrival? The Rev. R. S. F. writes me, that he had been three times the subject of the first of the two methods: the operator was Mr. Stone, Lecturer at the Marylebone Scientific Institution. The first two experiments were successful, the third failed. Then Mr. F. writes, "The only circumstance which I noticed (bearing upon the above question) in myself, and which I afterwards found tallied with the experience of others, was this: On the two occasions when I was affected, after about ten minutes the coin began to disappear from my sight, and to reappear a confused, brilliant substance, similar to those appearances which remain on the retina after one has been looking towards the sun for a few minutes, and I seemed for the moment to have fallen into a half-dreamy state; but in the subsequent part of the experiments, I appeared to myself to be in my ordinary state. On the third occasion, when the experiment failed with myself and with all the others, (which I think might be accounted for by the accidental irregularity of the proceedings,) I did not experience the sensations mentioned above." This account tallies with other evidence upon the point; a brief period of disturbed sensation, or threatening confusion, or loss of consciousness, passes over the patient. The wing of the unseen power, to speak figuratively, has cast its shadow upon him. It is evident that this transient psychical disturbance is the same phenomenon with that which Zschokke experienced whenever his seer-gift was manifested. The agency which thus can at pleasure be used to call forth trance-umbra, is the same which employed longer, or more intensely, produces perfect trance. The little dose thrilling through the system, without driving sense and apprehension from their usual seats, seems, as it were, to remove their fastenings; to throw up, as it were, the sashes of the body, so that the soul can now look forth and see, not as through a glass, darkly, but free to grasp directly things out of its corporeal tenement, whether of the nature of matter or mind.

But, at the same time, this same loosening of physical bonds renders the mind correspondingly denuded to aggressions from without. We have seen how strangely the entranced mind becomes sympathetically subject to the will, and the subject of the sensations of the person with whom it has been brought into mesmeric relation. But now a new feature, or one feebly manifested as yet in trance, but parallel to the influence of sympathy, displays itself. The person in trance-umbra is an absolute slave to the spoken, or even to the unexpressed "mental suggestions" of the operator. Sense, memory, judgment, give way at his word. The patient believes whatever he is told to believe,—that an apple is an orange,—that he himself is the Duke of Wellington,—that the operator standing before him is invisible to him,—and makes fruitless efforts to execute any voluntary movement the moment he is told he cannot. I will quote a passage, in illustration of the above, again from Mr. F.'s letter:—"After a quarter of an hour Mr. Stone came to us, and looked in our eyes for a few seconds, and desired us to close them. He then placed his thumb lightly on my forehead, and said, peremptorily, 'You cannot open your eyes.' I had great difficulty in doing so, but at last succeeded, with a violent struggle. After Mr. Stone had repeated the order or suggestion once or twice more, I was quite unable to open my eyes. Five out of the number, (about a dozen,) who sat down were affected, all more than myself. On a succeeding evening, however, Mr. Stone was able to proceed so far as to make me forget my name and address, by the simple assertion, 'You cannot remember your name,' &c., though he had before this just asked for them, and the answer was scarcely out of my mouth when he made me forget it. I think I never exerted my will more strongly than in trying to open my eyelids when they had been thus closed; but it appeared simply impossible to do this till the operator's magic 'All right,' immediately set them free. On several, who were highly susceptible, Mr. Stone proceeded with other experiments. A stick was said to be a rattlesnake, and believed to be so. The room became a garden at his command, with wild beasts in it. One was set a-fishing and snow-balling; another taken up in a balloon. A still more curious instance was when the subject was told that he was in the dark, and a candle was passed before his eyes, almost close enough to singe the eyebrows, without producing any visual impression on the eye, though the party operated on said he felt the warmth of it."

I have preferred giving additional and unpublished evidence of the wonderful control which can thus be "suggestively" exercised over the belief of a person in trance-umbra, to quoting Professor Gregory's most interesting cases, for which the reader must consult his recent valuable work. In the sixth letter in the present volume, (that on Somnambulism,) I have exemplified the manifestation of the same phenomena in the case of the sleep-walker Negretti. As a large number of persons can be thrown easily into the state of trance-umbra; and as then they are totally in the power of the operator, it is surely most desirable that this and the parallel easily induced conditions of the frame should be made subjects of careful observation and study by many competent persons, in order that the conditions necessary to their induction may be exactly ascertained, and made public, for the protection of society.

Of equal interest is the discovery that clairvoyance may be manifested in the state of trance-umbra. Major Buckley is spoken of by Professor Gregory as a gentleman possessing mesmerising force of a remarkable quality and degree. It appears that he had been long in the habit of producing magnetic sleep, and clairvoyance in the sleep, before he discovered that, in his subjects, the sleep might be dispensed with. Dr. Gregory gives the following account of his present method:—

"Major B. first ascertains whether his subjects are susceptible, by making, with his hand, passes above and below their hands, from the wrist downwards. If certain sensations, such as tingling, numbness, &c., are strongly felt, he knows that he will be able to produce the magnetic sleep. But to ascertain whether he can obtain conscious clairvoyance, he makes slow passes from his own forehead to his own chest. If this produce a blue light in his face, strongly visible, the subject will probably acquire conscious clairvoyance. If not, or if the light be pale, the subject will only become clairvoyant in the sleep, (that is, when in perfect trance.) Taking those subjects who see a very deep blue light, he continues to make passes over his own face, and also over the object—a box or a nut, for instance—in which written or printed words are enclosed, which the clairvoyante is to read. Some subjects only require a pass or two to be made: others require many. They describe the blue light as rendering the box or nut transparent, so that they can read what is inside. This reminds us of the curious fact mentioned by Von Reichenbach, that bars of iron or steel, seen by conscious sensitives, without any passes, shining in the dark with the Od glow, appeared to them transparent like glass. If too many passes are made by Major B., the blue light becomes so deep that they cannot read, and some reverse passes must be made to render the colour of the light less deep. Major Buckley has thus produced conscious clairvoyance in eighty-nine persons, forty-four of whom have been able to read mottoes contained in nutshells purchased by other parties for the experiments. The longest motto thus read contained ninety-eight words." "A lady, one of Major Buckley's waking clairvoyantes, read one hundred and three mottoes contained in nuts in one day, without a pass being made on that occasion. In this and in many other cases, the power of reading through nuts, boxes, and envelopes, remained, when once induced, for about a month, and then disappeared. The same lady, after three months, could no longer read without passes; and it took five trials fully to restore the power. This may be done, however, immediately by inducing the mesmeric sleep and clairvoyance in that state, when the subjects, in the hands of Major Buckley, soon acquire the power of waking clairvoyance."

But stranger things remain behind—corollaries, however, of the preceding, yet which eclipse these wonders, if possible. For a knowledge of these, I am exclusively indebted to Professor Gregory's recent publication, and I give them on his authority.

If the looking intently upon a piece of metal will produce trance and trance-umbra, why should not the account of the Egyptian boy-seers be correct? If their performance be often a trick, may not the protracted gaze on the black spot in their hand sometimes render them waking clairvoyantes? and why, on the same showing, might not the gazing upon magic crystals or mirrors of jet occasionally have thrown the already awe-struck and fitly disposed lookers on them into the state in which either the magician at their side might compel *suggestively* images into their fancy, or they, acting for themselves, have exercised independent ultravision, retrovision, prevision? Why, again, should not simple concentration of thought upon one uninteresting idea convert a susceptible subject into a soothsayer? Then read the following facts recorded by Dr. Gregory; I at least do not question their fidelity.

"Mr. Lewis possesses at times the power of spontaneous clairvoyance, by simple concentration of thought. He finds, however, that gazing into a crystal substance produces the state of waking clairvoyance in him much sooner and more easily. On one occasion, being in a house in Edinburgh with a party, he looked into a crystal, and saw in it the inhabitants of another house at a considerable distance. Along with them he saw two strangers, entire strangers to him. These he described to the company. He then proceeded to the other house, and there found the two strangers whom he had described."

"On another occasion he was asked to inspect a house and family, quite unknown to him, in Sloane Street,

Chelsea, he being in Edinburgh with a party. He saw in the crystal the family in London; described the house, and also an old gentleman very ill or dying, and wearing a peculiar cap. All was found to be correct, and the cap was one which had lately been sent to the old gentleman. On the same occasion Mr. Lewis told a gentleman present that he had lost or mislaid a key of a very particular shape, which he, Mr. L., saw in the crystal. This was confirmed by the gentleman, a total stranger to Mr. Lewis."

"Sistimus hic tandem."

I think that I have tolerably succeeded in establishing the thesis with which these Letters started, that every superstition is based on a truth; and I am in hopes that the mass of evidence which I have adduced—the very variety of the phenomena described, joined to their mutual coherence—the theoretical consistency of the whole, as if it were truly a vast body of living science, and not the "disjecta membra" of a dream—will remove every remaining shade of doubt among candid readers, that these inquiries are not less sound than they are curious.

CONCLUSION.

An acquaintance with the facts which it has been the object of the foregoing pages to assemble, and to render into philosophy, suggests one or two serious reflections.

We have seen the different results which have ensued when these facts have emerged into day in times of ignorance and in times of enlightenment. On the first occasion they were viewed with terror—became instruments of superstition—were used for bad designs—and even originated new forms of crime, before which common sense fled, and justice became blind and iniquitous. On the latter—I speak of the reception of these facts towards and in the present century—they were recognised by one after another of the most sagacious observers of nature; by Jussieu, for instance, and by Cuvier, to begin with; and gradually by an increasing host of candid, well-informed, and able followers, as forming a part of natural science, and as susceptible of important applications.

He is ranked among the wisest of mankind, who announced that "knowledge is power." Divine Wisdom goes further, and reveals to us that knowledge is a good and virtuous thing, while ignorance is stamped by the same seal as sinful; or how otherwise can we interpret the course of history and human experience, which proves that, by the very constitution of our being, and the laws impressed upon the moral and physical world, increase of knowledge contributes to promote general and individual well-doing and happiness, while ignorance never fails to be followed by the contrary penal consequences? Therefore it is that those who unite good intentions and good principles, with sound and well-cultivated abilities —in other words the truly wise—humbly deem, that among the most acceptable offerings to our common Maker must be diligence in exploring *all* the sources of knowledge which he has placed within our reach, (which were hidden only that we might seek for them,) so as to unveil more and more of the forces and powers of nature, in publishing the same abroad, that all may profit by them, and in striving to bend their agencies towards good, and high, and useful purposes.

THE END.

www.ingramcontent.com/pod-product-compliance
Lightning Source LLC
LaVergne TN
LVHW010245110826
845151LV00004B/1401

9781425523251